ALASKA

By the staff of Editions Berlitz

How to use our guide

- A **general introduction** by Douglas Ward, Director of the Cruise Passengers' Club International, gives you the feel of Alaska and British Columbia.

- Everything you need to know about **choosing** the right ship starts on page 9.

- The complete **fleet** of ships serving Alaska and British Columbia with ports of departure and arrival and cruise duration are on pp. 10–11.

- The section **Know Before You Go** starting on p. 12 provides a rundown of practical information and advice for before you depart, items that may also influence your choice of ship or date.

- **Life Aboard** on p. 29 tells you what to expect on board in the way of facilities, activities and entertainment.

- The **Briefings** starting on p. 41 fill you in on the background story to Alaska and British Columbia, and explain what a glacier actually is.

- A description of the 12 major Alaskan and British Columbian **ports of call** begins on page 67, each with its own history and sightseeing sections and a round-up of important excursions from the port.

- Finally there is an **index** at the back of the book on pp. 159–160, situating the ports and points of excursion mentioned.

Printed in Switzerland by Weber S.A., Bienne.

Contents

Text: Jack Altman
Layout: Doris Haldemann
🌐 **Cartography:** Falk Verlag, Hamburg

Maps: Alaska and British Columbia p. 22–23; Vancouver p. 89
Photos: Cover Photo by courtesy of Holland America Line, pp. 5, 8, 18, 19, 34 Maximilien Bruggmann; pp. 30, 31, 70 PRISMA; pp. 15, 86, 111, 115, 128, 143, 147, 151, 155 KEY-color/ZEFA; p. 65 KEY-color Photri; pp. 27, 116, 125, 127 Spectrum Colour Library; p. 39, 135, 140, 149 Travel Pictures, Brussels; pp. 71, 75, 79, 83, 107 Schuster; pp. 90, 93, 95, 96, 99, 104 Robert Harding Picture Library; p. 91 Canadian Government Office of Tourism; pp. 103, 105 Prince Rupert Visitor's Bureau; pp. 119, 131 Alaska Tourist Office.

Acknowledgments

We would like to extend our thanks to Nicholas Campbell and Paulette Pratt for their help in the preparation of this guide. We are also grateful to the Alaska State Division of Tourism for their assistance, and to Douglas Ward for his advice.

Although we make every effort to ensure the accuracy of all the information in this book, changes occur incessantly. We cannot therefore take responsibility for facts, prices, addresses and circumstances in general that are constantly subject to alteration. Our guides are updated on a regular basis as we reprint, and we are always grateful to readers who let us know of any errors, changes or serious omissions they come across.

Reviving a colourful tradition… today's descendant of the Tlingit tribe in full ceremonial garb.

General Introduction

by Douglas Ward, Director,
Cruise Passengers' Association International

In this over-civilized world of ours, there's something exhilarating and at the same time reassuring in the very idea of Alaska, still the last frontier, the last great wilderness to challenge the American pioneering spirit.

Exhilarating for the sheer adventure of the untamed north, its glaciers, vast forests and mountain torrents, but also for the sturdy breed of men and women who have settled there.

Reassuring for the knowledge that America's ecological awakening came in time to keep the great oil bonanza of the Trans-Alaska Pipeline from totally disrupting the natural environment and the ancient lands of the Indians, Eskimos and Aleuts.

Alaska's 586,412 square miles of rugged, beautiful country is spread over four time zones and is bounded by a coastline 33,000 miles long. *"Alyeska"* means "The Great Land"—and Alaska lives up to the name in almost every way. Apart from its population, that is–there are barely 400,000 people in the entire state.

Yes, Alaska is very big. Everything that makes and occasionally breaks it is on a similar scale. The gold rush at the end of the 19th century centred around what was at the time, in terms of daily tonnage, the largest mine in the world—the Alaska-Juneau. The earthquake that devastated south-central Alaska in 1964 ran up a frightening 8.5 on the Richter scale—San Francisco's was 8.25. Luckily, the pipeline coming out at Valdez wasn't in operation at the time, although it has been constructed to resist earthquakes. The pipeline now draws on reserves of nearly ten thousand million barrels of crude oil, nearly half the total reserves of the rest of the continental U.S.—the part usually referred to, with a bit of a smirk, as the "lower 48".

And the farmers won't let you forget about their great Matanuska Valley cabbages. Cabbages? Yes, cabbages. At the experimental agricultural area north-east of Anchorage, by some freak combination of prolonged sub-arctic sun and peculiar soil conditions, they produce cabbages so big that you need a wheelbarrow to take one home.

But Alaska is awesome not only because of its size, but also because of its beauty. It has a diversity of landscape and climate that surprises those unenlightened of us stuck with the image of Eskimos and deep snows.

Along the coastline on either side of Juneau, the south-eastern Panhandle is not at all Arctic in climate. Three-quarters of the region is covered by the Tongass National Forest—Sitka spruce and western hemlock conifers, but also the lovely red and yellow cedar, alder and black cottonwood.

The Western region, which takes in the Alaskan Peninsula and the Aleutian and Pribilof Islands, has a climate that is not what they call these days "people-friendly". Only the robust Aleuts and a few Yup'ik Eskimos can take—and even seem to enjoy—the foggy, wet and windy weather. The Interior covers a whole range of extremes, with summers as hot and dry as a desert, and winters much as you would expect.

It is the state's fifth region, the Arctic, that truly represents Alaska as a bleak wasteland of permanently frozen soil (permafrost). There, the only thing that doesn't freeze in the winter is the vodka.

The North Slope is where they found the oil. Like the gold of the 19th century, it took the discovery of treasure in the earth to lure others besides the state's perennial bunch of romantic nature-lovers. The men—and women—who braved the Far North's elements to drill for oil, then construct and maintain an 800-mile pipeline came mostly with oil-industry experience from the southern and western states.

Some save up as much of their high wages as the high cost of living will allow, taking it back after a few years to a less adventurous, but warmer, life in the lower 48. Many others get a taste for the challenge and stay, unable any more to settle for the easy life. You won't meet many softies in Alaska.

Alongside them is a solid core of native peoples—Eskimos, Aleuts and Indians—who were there before the oil and before the gold, and who were nature-lovers not out of nostalgia for some long-lost era, but out of simple necessity.

The old native culture has been much eroded by modern civilization, but you'll still come across the craftwork of wood-carving, ivory jewellery, basketware and the great handknitted woollen sweaters with the ancient totemic patterns.

British Columbia combines for Canada the great resources of a beautiful backwoods wilderness with the modern dynamism of Vancouver and charming anomaly of its Old English capital, Victoria. B.C. also offers the challenge of the wild outdoors, but with a gentler edge.

With some faster diplomatic and financial footwork, British Columbia might have swallowed up Alaska. As it is, they share a taste for first-class seafood and freshwater fish—salmon, trout, crab and jumbo shrimp. Tastier than 10 billion barrels of crude oil any day.

Travelling by cruise ship is a wonderful vacation in itself and is also the most comfortable way to be introduced to the many charms of Alaska and British Columbia. As your ship gently slips into glacier-packed passages, you can witness the dramatic spectacle of icebergs breaking up, as well as glimpsing playful seals and the graceful movement of whales clustered together.

Only here can you stand on a glacier, climb a mountain, fish in a romantic fjord, dance with Indians, pan for gold, gorge yourself at a salmon bake, photograph a bald eagle or grizzly bear, and watch whales... all this even in *one day*. Such is Alaska.

Fishing for salmon: the jogging gear may be new but the method goes back centuries.

Choosing Your Cruise

Your choice of ship will depend on several factors, including price. Here are some for consideration.

Alaska cruises offer spectacular scenery, and include one or more visits to glacial areas. Some cruises will include numerous glaciers, each one seemingly more breathtaking than the one before. Indeed, some of the most fascinating sights await the cruise passenger opting for a cruise that extends as far as to the north as possible. It is important to look at the brochures and study the various itineraries well. Your choice will depend on whether you wish to see more natural scenery and wildlife, or more ports. Cruises last from 3 to 18 days, so somewhere there is a cruise that's just right for *you*.

Because Alaska cruises are traditionally taken by those who enjoy nature and scenery rather than sunshine and sand, the age range of participants tends to be of middle age and above. That does not mean young people do not go to Alaska—simply that, for many, it is not an automatic choice as a vacation destination. Thus, activities and entertainment on Alaska cruise ships point towards the upper age bracket, with early mornings and not a lot of late-night activity.

However, Alaska cruises are highly recommended for families with young children, because of the unique educational experience and contact with nature they offer. Thus, parents should choose a ship that caters for children as well as themselves. Some ships don't.

Throughout the years, the most popular cruise has been one of 7 days. Alaska cruises are no exception, with the majority of lines operating 7-day runs from a port such as Vancouver. However, several ships give cruises of 10-14 days, starting from ports south of Vancouver like Seattle or San Francisco. Some lines offer short cruises that are in effect 3- or 4-day segments of a 7-day vacation.

Those who have been to Alaska before, perhaps on a short cruise, would be wise to consider one of the longer, in-depth cruises that go to more northerly destinations. And for those who are really adventurous, there's even a cruise expedition to the fascinating Aleutian Islands, including a crossing of the Arctic Circle.

Medium and large cruise ships (those over 20,000 tons) are sometimes unable to dock at small Alaskan ports, which means a short "tender" ride from ship to shore. This is fairly simple, but means that you will get a little less time ashore than if you were to dock. Large ships sometimes have a more impersonal atmosphere, but provide extensive facilities, more space and a greater choice of food.

Small ships (those under 20,000 tons) will be able to dock in most

Alaskan ports. Since fewer passengers are carried, the atmosphere is likely to be more intimate, although facilities available are generally less sophisticated.

One cruise ship is equipped to take vehicles, thus providing its "upstairs" passengers with the opportunity to experience Alaska to the fullest while enjoying a luxury cruise for part of the journey.

Cruising to Alaska is a relaxing and rewarding experience. No matter which ship or cruise you decide on, once you've experienced the fresh air and calm seas of this enchanting region, you'll want more.

Alaska Cruise Fleet

Line/Operator	Ship	From/To	No. of days
Costa Cruises	*Daphne*	Vancouver/ Vancouver	7
Cunard Line	*Cunard Princess*	Vancouver/Whittier	7
		Whittier/Vancouver	7
Cunard/NAC	*Sagafjord*	Vancouver/Whittier	11
		Whittier/Vancouver	10
Exploration Cruises	*Great Rivers Explorer*	Seattle/Ketchikan	11
		Ketchikan/Skagway	11
		Ketchikan/Skagway	5
		Skagway/Ketchikan	4
		Ketchikan/Ketchikan	8
	Majestic Explorer	Seattle/Ketchikan	11
		Ketchikan/Seattle	11
		Ketchikan/Ketchikan	7
		Ketchikan/Skagway	3
		Skagway/Ketchikan	4
	North Star	Seattle/Ketchikan	11
		Ketchikan/Seattle	10
		Prince Rupert/ Prince Rupert	8
		Prince Rupert/Skagway	5
		Skagway/Prince Rupert	4

Line/Operator	Ship	From/To	No. of days
Holland America Westours	*Nieuw Amsterdam*	Vancouver/Vancouver	7
		Vancouver/Juneau	3
		Juneau/Vancouver	4
	Noordam	Vancouver/Vancouver	7
		Vancouver/Juneau	3
		Juneau/Vancouver	4
	Rotterdam	Vancouver/Vancouver	7
		Vancouver/Juneau	3
		Juneau/Vancouver	4
Princess Cruises	*Island Princess*	Vancouver/Vancouver	7
	Pacific Princess	Seattle/Seattle	7
	Royal Princess	San Francisco/ San Francisco	10
	Sun Princess	Vancouver/Vancouver	7
Regency Cruises	*Regent Sea*	Vancouver/Whittier	7
		Whittier/Vancouver	7
Royal Cruise Line	*Golden Odyssey*	Vancouver/Whittier	7
		Whittier/Vancouver	7
Royal Viking Line	*Royal Viking Star*	San Francisco/ Vancouver	11
		Seattle/Seattle	10
Sitmar Cruises	*Fairsea*	Seattle/Seattle	10
	Fairsky	San Francisco/ San Francisco	12
Society Expeditions	*Society Explorer*	Kushiro/Nome	18
Sundance Cruises	*Stardancer**	Vancouver/Vancouver	7
		Vancouver/ Skagway (Haines)	4
		Skagway (Haines)/ Vancouver	3
World Explorer Cruises	*Universe*	Vancouver/Vancouver	14

* ship carries cars and RVs (recreational vehicles)

Know Before You Go

Accommodation

Standard Features

Think of a reduced version of an average hotel room and you'll have an idea of how your shipboard accommodation will look. Ships necessarily have space limitations, and therefore use space with the utmost efficiency. Almost all cabins will have the following features:

- two beds, or a lower and upper berth (plus, possibly, another one or two upper "pullman" berths)
- private bathroom and shower (higher-priced de luxe staterooms and suites often feature full-size bath tubs, or even a whirlpool bath)
- multi-channel radio, with television on some ships (although only closed-circuit television can be used at sea) or video equipment
- individual room-temperature controls

Cabin Availability

Although you may request a specific cabin when you book your cruise, many lines now designate cabins only at the point of embarkation. However, they will guarantee the rate and cabin category you request, which is a help.

You can always ask your cruise/travel agent the square footage of the cabin category you have selected. This will give you some idea of your cabin space.

Room with a View?

Outside staterooms have large picture windows or portholes with a sea view, and are thus more expensive than inside (no window) cabins. Check the deck plan carefully, however, for some outside cabins could well have a view of a lifeboat, running track or someone else's private sun deck!

If you are a first-time cruiser, an outside cabin is preferable by far. Without a porthole or window, you may find it difficult to orient yourself or gauge the weather.

However, accommodation in the centre of the ship does give a more stable ride. Here, you are relatively free from any vibration, which is directed mainly towards the stern.

Other Points to Consider

Cabin categories and prices are determined by size, location and view.

Generally, the larger the ship, the greater the accommodation space. Newer ships tend to offer more public room space, to the detriment of cabin space, and although the cabin space is designed and used in a more efficient manner, it seems to decrease in direct proportion to the newness of the vessel.

Decide how much you can afford to spend, including air fare (if applicable) and on-board expenses, as this will determine the cabin categories available to you. However, take the most expensive cabin you can afford, as you will be spending some time there. If it is too small (and most cabins are small), it will not be as comfortable as your own bedroom at home and "cabin fever" can develop, with the result that your cruise may not live up to your expectations.

This is not so much of a problem if the ship offers an extensive (port-a-day) itinerary, since you will spend less time in your cabin than if the itinerary includes fewer ports and more days at sea.

So, consult the deck plan carefully, taking note of cabin and public room locations in relation to stairways, elevators, restaurants and outdoor deck areas, and bear in mind the following:

Closet space is limited on ships, so if you are taking an extended cruise, make sure that there will be sufficient space for the amount of luggage you may wish to take.

Double beds are a rarity on cruise ships. Honeymooners (and the romantics among us) would be wise to check their availability at the time of booking.

Electric current on most cruise ships is the standard American 110-volt/60-cycle A.C., while some European-owned ships have both 110- and 220-volt outlets. Normally, electrical appliances may be used only if they operate on 110 volts A.C., so ask your cruise/travel agent before taking appliances more powerful than an electric razor, such as a high-wattage hair-dryer.

The food is the same, whatever accommodation you choose—from the most expensive down to the cheapest—and is eaten in the same restaurant.

A final note:

Your cabin is one of the first things you'll want to see when you board your ship, Therefore, think carefully when making a choice—if the ship is full, it may prove difficult to change your accommodation or "upgrade" your cabin to a higher price category.

Booking

Cruise lines offer several booking options, and these can sometimes be tailored to best suit your needs. Cruises are usually offered either as a combination air/sea package with an all-inclusive price or simply the cruise itself.

The Alaska cruise season is relatively short, and the peak weeks of July and August sell out rapidly. So, see your cruise/travel agent and make your reservations at the earliest opportunity, in order to obtain the cabin grade of your choice.

Cruise Tariffs

Prices quoted in cruise brochures are valid at the time of printing. All cruise lines reserve the right to change prices in the event of increases in tariffs, rates of exchange, costs of fuel or any other costs beyond their control.

Your cruise/travel agent will have the correct prices to hand when you book, and you will receive confirmation of these when you have made your reservation and forwarded the deposit or final payment.

All fares must be paid in full before departure.

What Your Fare Includes

– Ocean transportation and accommodation
– Meals, snacks and entertainment on board
– Use of health and fitness facilities and sports equipment (apart from skeet shooting)
– Ship-to-shore launch (where applicable)
– Airport-seaport transfer (with possible exception of Seattle-Vancouver coach connection)

The other side of Alaska—a charming tapestry of leaves.

Not Included
– Port taxes
– Shore excursions
– Drinks
– Laundry and dry cleaning
– Hairdressing, massage and beauty treatment

Port Taxes
These are assessed by individual port authorities and will be indicated on the tariff for each itinerary. They are due at the time of final payment. In most cases, they will be included on your final payment invoice from the cruise line or your cruise/travel agent.

Airport Transfer
The cost of transportation from airport to cruise ship and back will in most cases be included in your air-sea package. It is advisable, however, to check with the cruise/travel agent before you go.

Cancellation
All cruise lines issue notices regarding cancellation, refunds and cancellation insurance. If you don't turn up for the cruise, you normally forfeit any monies paid.

Clothing

When thinking of a cruise to Alaska, "be prepared" is the best maxim. Although you'll want to keep your luggage to a minimum, bear in mind that the climate in Alaska, even in the summertime, can turn from warm and mild to rainy, misty and miserable within an hour or so. As a rule, summer days are dry, with intermittent spells of misty and cloudy weather. You'll find a temperature chart on page 28 to give you an idea of what to expect.

Dress On Board
There are two occasions during your cruise when formal or semi-formal attire is required. These are on the second night, for the Captain's Cocktail Party and Welcome Aboard Dinner, and on the night before last, when the Captain's Farewell Dinner and Gala Midnight Buffet are held.

The first and last nights of any cruise are strictly informal, but there may well be special "theme" nights during the rest of the cruise, when you may wish to wear something appropriate in order to participate in the spirit of the occasion. Examples of these are: French Night, Red, White and Blue Night, Italian Night, etc. Ask your cruise/travel agent for a list of current "theme" nights planned for your cruise. (See *Fancy Dress*, p. 32)

For women, sportswear, medium-weight knits, slacks and pant-suits are ideal shipboard wear, while men should take a blazer and sports jacket or two, plus some sweaters for those cool Alaska evenings. In addition, as a general rule, men should wear a jacket for dinner in the dining room.

Pack at least one bathing suit for the ship's heated swimming pool (or for use in the sauna or hot-tubs on some Alaska ships). And for those who are athletically inclined, remember to take a lightweight track suit or shorts and top for the running track and gymnasium.

What to Wear Ashore

For shore excursions in Alaska, it's best to use the "layered" approach. That means warm, comfortable clothing next to your body, plus a sweater and some protective outer wear that can be removed if it gets warm. If you are going on a "flightseeing" excursion, take a heavy-weight sweater and some outer wear—especially useful if you visit a glacier by helicopter and get out on the glacier itself. In this case you will need your sunglasses, for the light is extremely bright on glaciers and at glacial faces.

Pack several sweaters, a parka-type jacket and raincoat for general wear, as well as a pair of gloves. A small umbrella might be a wise addition.

Shoes should be as comfortable as possible, especially if you intend to do a lot of walking and exploring. For those steep Alaska hillsides and mountains, a good pair of hiking boots are a worthwhile investment. Women are advised not to wear high-heeled shoes on board ship, except on formal nights. Also keep in mind that many Alaskan towns have few roads and uneven pavements, for which a pair of sneakers are advisable.

Packing Hints

There is normally no limit to the amount of personal baggage allowed on board cruise ships, but due to the rather limited closet space available on most ships, it is advisable to take only clothing, shoes and personal effects that you intend to use. Towels, soap and shower caps are provided by the ship.

When packing, remember to leave room for the local knitwear you'll be tempted to buy during your Alaskan cruise.

If you are travelling to or from the ship by air, the airline's baggage

allowance should be checked in advance through your cruise/travel agent.

It is important for all bags to be properly labelled, and tagged with the owner's name, ship, cabin number, sailing date and port of embarkation.

Liability for loss of or damage to luggage is limited by the passage contract. If you are not adequately covered, take out insurance for this purpose. The policy should extend from the date of departure until two or three days after your return home. Insurance coverage may be obtained from your cruise/travel agent or insurance agent.

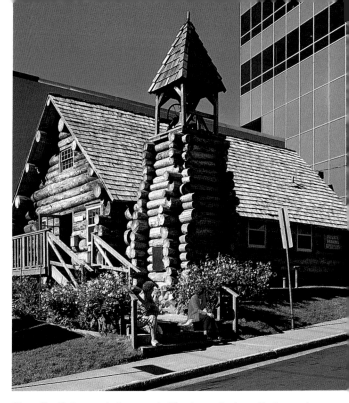

Naturally Alaska... a glacier untouched by time and a log cabin in an urban environment.

Communications

Ship-to-Shore Telephone

On most ships, you can call from your cabin (or the ship's Radio Room) to anywhere in the world while at sea via ship-to-shore telephone. This is effected in one of two ways: by radiotelephone—a slight to moderate background noise and echo may accompany your call—or by satellite, which is as clear as your own phone at home. The second is the more expensive of the two methods.

Each ship has a designated call sign, which is a combination of four letters, or letters and digits, and can be obtained from the cruise line. To receive a call during your cruise, simply give the call sign and name of the ship to anyone who will be contacting you in this way.

Other Means
Telegram and telex services also enable you to make contact speedily whenever necessary during your voyage. (See *Telegrams and Telex*, p.38)

Documents

Identity
Citizens of the United States and Canada are not required to carry passports or tourist cards, but are advised to take some documentary proof of citizenship, such as a voter's registration card, copy of a birth certificate or passport. All other passengers must possess a valid passport and any necessary visas when boarding. Foreigners resident in the U.S. must also carry their Alien Registration Card.

Visas
Non-U.S. citizens taking a cruise from a U.S. port must have a valid B-2 multiple-entry (visitor's) visa. U.S. citizens taking a cruise from a Canadian port will need to carry proof of citizenship. All others, except for British passport holders, will need to obtain a Canadian visa before taking a cruise from or to a Canadian port.

Embarkation/Disembarkation

Passengers are normally required to board their cruise ship about three hours before sailing. When you embark, you hand in your tickets and any other relevant documents and are given a personal Boarding Pass. This must be carried with you at all times when going ashore. It serves as identification as well as enabling you to reboard the ship. Embarkation is a smooth, rapid procedure.

During the final part of your cruise, the Cruise Director will give an informal talk on customs, immigration and disembarkation procedures. It is recommended that at least one member of each group attend this important talk, as this will help to simplify and speed up the procedure and avoid confusion at arrival time.

The night before your ship reaches its final destination, you will be given a customs form. Fill it out completely, and remember that any duty-free goods bought from the shop on board must be included, so save the receipts in case a customs officer asks to see them.

Your main baggage should be packed and placed outside your cabin the night before final arrival, on retiring, or at any rate no later than 4 a.m. It will be collected, placed in a central baggage area and unloaded on arrival. Remember to leave out any fragile items, together with the clothes you intend to wear for disembarkation. Anything left in your cabin at this point will be considered hand baggage, and must be carried by you when you disembark. Remember to claim any items you may have placed in the ship's safety deposit boxes, and leave your key behind when you depart. The ship will not be cleared by the authorities for passengers to proceed ashore until all baggage has been taken off and customs and/or immigration inspections or pre-inspections have been carried out on board.

In most ports, this normally takes two to three hours. For comfort and convenience, passengers are requested to remain in the public rooms or their cabins and to listen for announcements on disembarkation. You should not crowd the gangway or disembarkation areas.

After you have disembarked, you identify and collect your baggage on the pier before going through any main or secondary customs and/or immigration controls.

Excursions

Organized Tours

Excursions are organized by a cruise line's Shore Excursion Department in conjunction with local shore-based tour operators, and each cruise line acts purely as a sales agent on behalf of the shore tour operator. Tours are planned to highlight major sights of cultural, historic or scenic interest in any port, and are composed so as to provide the most practical, yet cost-efficient, method of transportation available.

Buses, rather than taxis, are used for many tours because they allow a tour operator to select the best available guides (i.e. those with the most thorough local knowledge and who are competent, reliable and fluent in English).

Some cruise lines pre-sell tour packages to passengers prior to sailing. Please bear in mind that, generally, these cannot be exchanged on board for other tours, credited, or refunded.

If you have prebooked shore excursions (either individually or as a package), please remember to check at the Tour Office on board to make sure that there are no modifications or cancellations of the shore excursion programme due to changes in itinerary, times of arrival and departure, or local conditions.

Lift-Off in Alaska

There is no more exciting experience in Alaska than "lifting off" in a float plane or helicopter, and heading for the nearby mountains and glaciers. The view is breathtaking, and landing high up on a mountain lake or on the surface of a glacier adds to the exhilaration. For photographers, it's a great way to add dimension by capturing the splendour of Alaska from aloft.

But remember: book any flight excursions at the earliest opportunity as they are limited in number and availability.

Cancelling Excursions

If you purchase tickets for shore excursions and then for some reason change your mind, there may be a "penalty". Many cruise lines require 24 hours' notice to cancel, since the Tour Manager must radiotelephone "final numbers" to the next port to secure transport, guides and any food required.

Independent Travel Ashore

You are, of course, under no obligation to take part in the shore excursion programme—it is there should you wish to avail yourself of its advantages. Passengers are free to go ashore on their own in all ports of call in Alaska. The Tour Office can handle enquiries, but cannot make individual arrangements for tours, although such things as rented cars or fishing-boat charters can often be made via the Tour Manager on board. Again, the earlier the better. (See *Reservations*, p. 25)

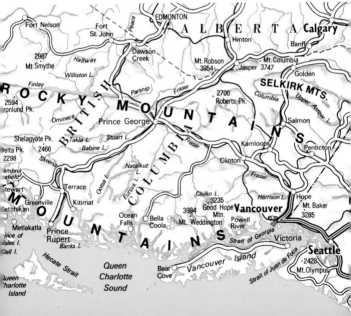

Health Tips

Invigorating Alaska

Even a spell of rain or cooler weather in Alaskan waters should not discourage you from getting out on deck. The sea air there is invigorating, and will do you the world of good.

Seasickness

All modern cruise ships are equipped with stabilizing "fins" that are pushed out into the water if a ship starts to roll, and can be recessed into the ship's side when not in use. These fins counteract more than 80 per cent of the roll of a ship. In any case, motion sickness—which used to be a common problem on the high seas—is relatively uncommon in the smooth sailing waters of Alaska and the Inland Passage.

If you do suffer from seasickness, however, help is at hand. All cruise ships have a fully equipped medical facility, including one or more doctors and a nursing staff. Seasickness tablets are available on most ships from a room steward. (See *Medical Services*, p. 35)

And the tranquillizing effect of a good massage can be a delightful form of preventive medicine at the first sign of queaziness.

Money Matters

Onboard Transactions

All transactions aboard Alaska cruise ships are in U.S. dollars. If you join or leave your ship in Vancouver—or go ashore anywhere in British Columbia—remember that the local currency there is the Canadian dollar. You may find that U.S. dollars get a less advantageous exchange rate if used directly in the shops.

Personal cheques are not usually accepted on board, but traveller's cheques (generally, at least those issued by U.S. banks) and major credit cards can be used for on-board purchases and transactions.

Currency Exchange

If you happen to have with you foreign currency, and want to change it, this may have to be done at a bank during one of the port visits—not all cruise ships have currency exchange facilities.

Pets

No pets are carried by Alaskan cruise ships.

Reservations

Dining Room

Once on board, take care of your dining room and sitting confirmation, if this has not already been done by your cruise/travel agent. After you have boarded, the *maître d'* will be in attendance outside the dining room or in one of the main public rooms to handle all passenger dining requests. Remember to state your preference for a smoking or non-smoking section, and to reconfirm any special dietary wishes.

Those who are into health foods should note that ship food is usually generously doused with salt, and vegetables are often cooked in sauces containing butter, milk and sugar. A word with the *maître d'* may avert problems at mealtimes. He should be able to order plainly cooked foods for you. (See *Special Requirements*, below)

Few ships offer tables for two in their dining rooms (upmarket ships are the exception), the norm being tables for four, six or eight. If you specifically request a table for two at the time of booking, confirm this once you are on board. (See *Which Sitting?*, p. 33)

Shipboard Services

Should you wish to be thoroughly pampered during your cruise and would like a massage, manicure or hair treatment, make an appointment at the appropriate place as soon as you board, as these are specialized services with limited personnel, and can soon become fully booked.

Passes for Visitors

If you want to organize a Bon Voyage Party or any other form of "send-off" celebration, notify your cruise/travel agent in advance, so that he can arrange passes for visitors.

Passengers wishing to invite visitors aboard in any port of call—or making their own arrangements involving bookings of any kind—should do this through the cruise/travel agent well in advance of the sailing date.

Special Requirements

Dietary

Passengers who are on any kind of restricted or special diet—such as vegetarian, no-salt, kosher or macrobiotic—should advise the cruise line at the time of booking. This will give adequate time for special dietary needs to be catered for, wherever possible.

Medical

Anyone who is disabled or suffering from an illness should indicate this when booking the cruise. This applies particularly to passengers with medical conditions that might require special, or unusual, medication or treatment.

Taking Pictures

Alaska is one of the most photogenic regions in all the world, with its deep-blue waters, blue-white glaciers, fabulous scenery and unusual wildlife. Through your photographs you can relive your Alaska cruise experience and share it with others.

Before taking your cruise, you should register your photographic equipment with your local customs office, as this will save you the embarrassment on your return of having to verify where it was purchased. This is especially true if you have the latest equipment. Take plenty of film with you, as film in Alaska is expensive, and the more unusual types may not be readily available.

Although you are on vacation, remember that the local inhabitants are not. Indians and Eskimos do not always enjoy being photographed as a sightseeing oddity, and some are superstitious about having their pictures taken. So ask permission beforehand. Politeness pays, and they will better respect you for your consideration.

Tipping

Tipping is a matter of personal consideration that many find awkward. Use the information given here as a guideline, and add your own good judgement.

On some ships, suggestions regarding tips are subtly given, while on others, Cruise Directors sometimes get carried away with the tipping message and are far too dictatorial. The "standard" for Alaska is:

Waiter—$2.50-$3 per day, Busboy—$1.25-$1.50 per day, Steward—$2.50-$3 per day.

Any other gratuities should be given according to services rendered, just as you would in any first-class hotel, for example, to the wine waiter, *maître d'*, barman or any other person who has been of particular help in making your cruise an enjoyable experience.

Envelopes for tipping are available at the Purser's Office.

More than just a family tree, the totem pole provides a fascinating testimony to Indian culture.

Weather

Glaciers don't necessarily mean icy weather – certainly not in the summer, when you have a succession of pleasantly mild and sunny days. But it can sometimes turn from clear to cloudy and you might experience the occasional shower or bout of drizzly weather. The chart below gives average daily temperatures from April to September.

		April	May	June	July	August	Sept.
Vancouver	C°	9	13	16	18	18	14
	F°	48	55	61	64	64	57
Anchorage	C°	2	5	12	14	14	9
	F°	36	41	54	57	57	48

Wheelchair Passengers

Cruise lines, port authorities, airlines and travel agents are becoming increasingly aware of the needs of the disabled. Unfortunately, several structural problems lie in the very design of passenger ships, which obviously must be constructed to keep out water. Consequently, raised "lips" are put at strategic locations, such as cabin doorways and exit pathways.

Bathroom doorways are particularly troublesome and so, often, is their position within cabins. Consider, too, that bathrooms on most ships are small and crammed full of plumbing fixtures at odd angles, totally unhelpful to those having to negotiate access from the confines of a wheelchair. To make matters worse, many cabin doorways are just not wide enough to accept even a standard-size wheelchair.

More and more ships however, have built or converted a number of specially fitted "access" cabins. To enable wheelchair passengers to get to outdoor areas, special ramps have been put in place, while on some ships portable ramps are kept for movement to awkward areas.

One of the main problems of "access" cruising in Alaska, apart from choosing the right ship, is that of actually getting off and on at each port. This is relatively easy when the ship docks alongside, but can be something of an ordeal if the ship lies at anchor and a motor launch is necessary to reach the shore.

It is thus imperative to read the cruise brochures carefully, and to ask your cruise/travel agent to give details of facilities on board for disabled passengers. He can also find out about the docking, anchor and launch arrangements for the cruise, as well as following up all other arrangements necessary for disabled passengers.

Life Aboard

Air Conditioning	Medical Services
Barber Shop/Beauty Salon	Movies
Bon Voyage Parties	Nautical Notes
Cabin Security	News and Sports Bulletins
Casino	Purser's Office
Cruise Director and Staff	Religious Services
Deck Chairs	Room Service
Drinks	Safety Aboard Ship
Entertainment	Sauna
Fancy Dress	Ship's Photographers
Fitness Facilities	Shopping
Launches	Shore Tours
Library	Sports Facilities
Lost and Found	Swimming Pools
Mail	Telegrams and Telex
Maître d'	Telephone
Massage	Tour Office
Meals	Twenty-Four-Hour Clock
That Famous Cruise Cuisine	Valet Service
Which Sitting?	Valuables
The Captain's Table	Variety Shows
Informal Eating	Visitors
Midnight Buffet	Wine and Liquor

Air Conditioning. On all modern cruise ships, cabin temperature is regulated by individually controlled thermostats, so that you can adjust the temperature in your cabin to your liking. Public room temperature is controlled automatically. European passengers should note that the air conditioning is normally kept at a much cooler temperature than they may be accustomed to.

Barber Shop/Beauty Salon. These will be found on board, and a charge is made for their services. It is advisable to make appointments as soon after boarding as possible.

Bon Voyage Parties. Liquor, ice, glasses, mixes, snacks and canapés for sailing parties must be ordered in advance through your cruise/travel agent (service not available on all ships: see *Passes for Visitors*, p. 25)

Cabin Security. All cabins have keys, and it is recommended that you keep your cabin locked when you are not there. (See *Valuables*, p. 40.)

Casino. Most Alaska cruise ships have a casino, where blackjack, roulette and numerous slot machines are available when the ship is at sea. The casino will be closed while the ship is in port, in accordance with local regulations.

Cruise Director and Staff. The entire passenger entertainment programme is put together by the ship's Cruise Staff, under the guidance of the Cruise Director. This group of professionals is there to make your cruise as entertaining—and complete—as possible. A *Daily Programme*, placed under your cabin door each evening, lists the activities planned for the following day as well as giving up-to-date information on all services. The Cruise Staff Office is usually in the main lobby area.

The best of both fishing worlds: inland lake and a day's catch from coastal waters.

Deck Chairs. Deck chairs and cushions are available free of charge on most ships, from the duty deck steward. Specific locations cannot be reserved, except on ships where a charge is made.

Drinks. There will be plenty to choose from during your Alaska cruise. The ship may feature a special drink-of-the-day, and the bartenders will know just how to make almost any drink there is. Some ships also feature "hot toddies" such as hot buttered rum, for occasions when the weather outside turns cold.

The Alaskan run also provides a good opportunity to sample Scandinavian aquavit, a particularly heartwarming drink to take while watching the glaciers and icebergs.

Entertainment. Live entertainment is a major feature of the cruise experience, with cabaret acts scheduled most evenings. Bands provide lively and sentimental music for dancing, and solo instrumentalists offer a relaxing background in the ship's intimate bars and lounges.

Other forms of entertainment include games, quizzes, movies, sports tournaments, bingo and horse racing.

Fancy Dress. Many passengers participate in the Fancy Dress or Masquerade Night and dress in all sorts of oddities, competing for prizes given for the most creative and original costume made on board. What men may lack in original costumes they can make up for with their wives' cosmetics. Ensure that your costume is something you can sit down in.

Fitness Facilities. Most ships have some kind of fitness facilities. These may include a complete spa or, depending on the size of the vessel, one or more of the following: gymnasium, weight room, sauna, solarium, exercise room, exercise classes, jogging track, parcours, massage, swimming pool(s), whirlpool baths, nutrition counselling, herbal body wraps and scuba and snorkel instruction. For more information, check with your cruise/travel agent or, when on board, contact the Purser's Office or Cruise Director.

Launches. Covered motor launches are used when your ship is unable to berth at a cruise port. In such cases, a regular launch (tender) service will operate between ship and shore for the duration of the port call.

Library. Most cruise ships have a library where you can browse through a wide range of books, reference material and periodicals. A small deposit (refundable) is often required if you wish to take a book out of the library during the cruise.

Lost and Found. Contact the Purser's Office immediately if you lose or find something on the ship. Notices will also be posted on the bulletin board.

Mail. You can buy stamps and post letters on board. Mail will usually be landed by the ship's port agent just before the ship sails for the next port. Postcards and writing paper are available from the Writing Room, Library, Purser's Office or your room steward.

Maître d'. This is the man to turn to on matters concerning dining room arrangements. The *maître d',* just like the maître d'hotel in a conventional restaurant, will be able to deal with any special food needs you might have – and he can also help diplomatically if there's ever a problem with your neighbours at the table.

Massage. Make your appointments for massage as soon as possible after boarding, in order to get the time slot you want. Larger ships have more staff, and therefore more flexibility and choice.

Meals

That Famous Cruise Cuisine. Cruise ships have become justly famous for their food, both for the quality and quantity. You could eat yourself into oblivion, there's so much to choose from. (Incidentally, there is no truth to the rumour that sea air shrinks your clothes, although it does seem to encourage a healthy appetite.) For breakfast alone, many cruise ships boast as many as sixty items. And for dinner—well, there's almost anything you could wish for, within reason.

Although the food does vary from ship to ship, generally it is of the international gourmet style, at least comparable to the "banquet" food found in a first-class hotel. If you are not used to this type of eating, select your first few meals carefully and avoid rich sauces. Don't be surprised to hear that the restaurant on your ship, and possibly its staff, is run by an outside operator. It's all a question of economics.

If there are any special (gourmet or otherwise) dishes not listed on the ship's menu that you would like prepared for you, speak to the *maître d'* 24 hours in advance, and he will do his best to arrange something for you. Birthdays, anniversaries and other celebrations can be pleasantly enhanced in this way. (See *Reservations*, p. 25)

Especially abundant on the Alaska cruises are salmon, lobster, crab and all manner of high-quality, locally-caught seafood.

Which Sitting? Except for the more upmarket ships, on which all passengers dine at the same time, there are two sittings for meals taken in the dining room.

The first, or main sitting, is for those who like early dining, and do not wish to take a long time over a meal. The second, or late sitting, is for people who enjoy a leisurely meal. Those at the late sitting may not be hungry enough to participate in the midnight buffet, and could find that the better seats in the cinema and at the shows are taken by passengers at the earlier sitting. To get around this problem, some ships stage two performances nightly, one for each sitting.

As a rule, most ships request that you enter the dining room not more than 15 minutes after the meal has been announced, out of consideration for other passengers, your fellow table companions and the dining room staff.

The Captain's Table. The Captain normally occupies a large table in the centre of the dining room, seating eight or ten people. Passengers are usually picked for this table from the passenger list (or "commend" list), by the *maître d'*. The Captain may also have personal friends or company officials already picked out. If you are asked, it is gracious to accept, and you'll have the chance to ask all the questions you'd like to about shipboard life. The Captain will not attend when he is required on the bridge.

Informal Eating. Early risers will find coffee and tea readily available from 6 a.m. onwards. On most ships, breakfast and lunch may be taken *al fresco*, or buffet style, at an outside, or deck, café. This is ideal for those who do not wish to dress for the more formal atmosphere of the dining room, or wish to view the passing scenery more closely. You can also take breakfast in your cabin. In addition, most ships offer mid-morning bouillon and afternoon tea (at 4 p.m. in the British tradition), both a carry-over from the grand days of Trans-Atlantic steamship travel.

Midnight Buffet. On several nights of your cruise, there will be a Midnight Buffet—one of them perhaps supplemented with as many as a dozen beautifully-sculpted ice carvings. These may have been made from ice "captured" by an early-morning passenger/crew "ice retrieval party" in one of the glacial areas along the way. Even if you do not wish to take part in the special buffet event, do have a look—and take your camera to get some outstanding photographs.

Almost anywhere, downtown is in the shadow of the great outdoors.

Medical Services. A doctor and nursing staff are on board ship at all times. There may also be a fully equipped hospital in miniature. Standard fees are charged for treatment, as well as consultation. Most ships do not charge for seasickness tablets, but do so for injections.

Movies. First-run movies are shown each day in the ship's theatre (times are given in the *Daily Programme*), and are chosen for their suitability and general appeal. Ships without a theatre may have cabin television sets equipped for videos and closed-circuit programming.

Nautical Notes. Each area of a ship is known by a certain name, as the following diagram illustrates:

PORT SIDE

AFT   AMIDSHIP   FORWARD

STARBOARD

Some commonly used nautical terms are:

aft—the stern, or after end of the ship
alleyway—narrow passage or corridor
astern—at or towards the stern
beam—breadth of ship at its widest point (usually amidships)
bow—the forwardmost part of the vessel
bridge—the platform from which the ship is navigated and controlled
bulkhead—any upright wall-like partition in a ship
companionway—a stairway or ladder leading from one deck to another
deck—floor
draft (or *draught*)—the depth of a ship in the water
galley—kitchen
gangway/gangplank—link between ship and shore
head—toilet
helm—the apparatus by which the ship is steered
hold—the space for storing cargo
keel—the plate extending lengthwise along the centre of the ship's bottom
leeward—the side which is sheltered from the wind
log—daily record of a ship's speed and progress

port—to your left, facing forward

stabilizer—a retractable "fin" extended from either side of the ship for smoother sailing

starboard—to your right, facing forward

stern—the rearmost part of the vessel

windward—the side towards which the wind blows

A *navigational broadcast* is normally made once or twice daily, giving the ship's position, temperature and weather information. At twelve noon, while the ship is at sea, the ship's whistle may be sounded for testing purposes, and to give the correct time.

A *nautical mile* is one-sixtieth of a degree of the earth's circumference and is equal to 6,076.1 feet. It is 796.1 feet (or one-seventh) longer than a land mile.

A *knot* is a unit of speed measuring one nautical mile per hour. Thus, when a ship is doing 20 knots (never 20 knots per hour), it is travelling at 20 nautical miles per hour.

News and Sports Bulletins. Daily news and sports bulletins are posted at the Purser's Office or on the bulletin boards. They may also be found in the ship's library.

Purser's Office. Centrally located, this is the nerve centre for general shipboard information or onboard problems. Opening hours are posted outside the office, and given in the *Daily Programme*. On some ships the Purser's Office is open 24 hours a day.

Religious Services. Inter-denominational services are conducted on board, usually by the Captain. On some ships, special services are conducted by invited or travelling priests or rabbis.

Room Service. Beverages and snacks are available at specific hours. Liquor service is normally limited to the hours when the ship's bars are open. Your room steward will advise you of the range of services.

Safety Aboard Ship. Passenger safety is the highest priority of any cruise line. Crew members attend frequent emergency drills, lifeboat equipment is regularly checked and fire-detection devices, alarms and firefighting systems are installed throughout most ships. If you detect fire or smoke, you should immediately notify the first staff member you see. Use the nearest fire alarm box or telephone the bridge. You'll find the number in the ship's telephone directory, a copy of which will be in your cabin. It might be an idea to memorize it or note it down.

Lifeboat drill for passengers takes place within 24 hours of embarkation.

Sauna. Many ships have a sauna, usually small and compact, and it may be unisex. On some ships a small charge will be made for its use, especially when combined with a massage.

Ship's Photographers. Professional photographers are on board ship to take pictures of passengers throughout the cruise, including your arrival and main events. All photographs can be viewed without obligation to purchase. The colour and quality of these photographs are usually excellent, and they may prove to be worthwhile souvenirs. They are displayed on photo boards in the main foyer, or in a separate Photo Gallery.

Shopping. The gift shop/boutique/drugstore provides a selection of souvenirs, gifts, toiletries and duty-free items, as well as a stock of essentials. Opening hours will be posted at the store, and given in the *Daily Programme*.

Shore Tours. All tour departure times are posted on board at the Tour Office, printed in the *Daily Programme* and announced over the ship's P.A. system by Tour Office staff prior to tour departure. On many ships these announcements are not put through accommodation areas, in case passengers are sleeping. Be on time for tours, and remember to take your tickets with you.

On Alaska cruise ships, the Cruise Director or Tour Manager will give an audio-visual lecture on each of the ports of call, together with hints on shopping and local history and a description of the tours available. This is normally arranged the day after sailing. The Tour Manager knows his job, so don't be afraid to ask questions or seek advice.

When choosing your onshore excursions, check whether they leave you with any time to yourself—either for private shopping expeditions or for anything else you might feel like doing while the ship is in port. (See *Excursions*, p. 21)

Sports Facilities. Depending on their size, ships will offer a variety of sports facilities. Tournaments are normally arranged by the Cruise Staff. Check the *Daily Programme* for times. Facilities will include one or more of the following: badminton, basketball practice area, golf driving cage, horseshoes, jogging track, miniature golf putting green, paddle tennis, quoits, ring toss, shuffleboard, skeet shooting, table tennis, volleyball.

Swimming Pools. These may be indoors or outdoors and might well be closed in port because of local regulations. Hours of operation will be listed in the *Daily Programme*.

Telegrams and Telex. These can be taken to the Purser's Office or Radio Room for transmission.

Telephone. All cabins have internal telephones that enable you to call any other cabin or part of the ship. On most ships you may also call anywhere in the world via your cabin telephone, when the ship is at sea. When the ship is in port you must use shore telephone.

Tour Office. The Tour Office on board is responsible for all aspects of the shore excursion operation, although tour office staff do not normally act as guides or interpreters. The office also acts as a port information centre and can supply you with tourist literature. Payment for tours is normally done through a central room billing system, by cash, traveller's cheques or credit card. Please note that on most ships, personal cheques cannot be accepted. Make your reservations at the earliest opportunity in order to avoid disappointment for those tours which have limited participation (especially sail or flight tours).

Twenty-Four-Hour Clock. On some European-owned ships, the twenty-four-hour clock is standard, in keeping with the traditions of international travel. In spite of the initial strangeness of this system of time-telling, you will soon find it not only simple to use, but far less likely to lead to confusion.

Up to midday, the hours are shown as 01.00-12.00; from midday to midnight, they become 13.00-24.00. Thus, 14.00, for example equals 2 p.m., 15.20 equals 3.20 p.m., and so on.

A breathtaking mass of blue ice dwarfs everything in its path.

Valet Service. Available through your room steward or stewardess, this will include one or more of the following services, depending on your cruise ship: cleaning and pressing, dry cleaning, laundry. For a list of charges, see your room steward or stewardess.

Valuables. Any items of special value should be placed in the safety deposit boxes available at the Purser's Office. Access to your valuables can be made by arrangement during the cruise. Cruise lines are not responsible for money or valuables left in cabins. (See *Cabin Security*, p. 29)

Variety Shows. For a list of what's on, where, and when, consult your *Daily Programme* or telephone the Cruise Staff Office.

Visitors. On the day of embarkation, passengers may normally invite friends to come aboard before sailing for a "bon voyage" party. Announcements will be made when it is time for all visitors to leave.

Passengers may also invite guests on board for lunch or dinner in the different ports of call, if space is available. A charge is made. Advance warning is advisable, and you should make arrangements with the *maître d'* on board at the earliest opportunity. (See *Passes for Visitors*, p. 25)

Wine and Liquor. The price of drinks on board ship is below that of comparable drinks on land. This is because ships are able to use duty-free liquor items. Drinks may be ordered in the dining room, at any of the bars or from room service. In the dining room, you will also be able to order wine with your meals from an extensive wine list. If you would like wine with your dinner, try to place your order at lunchtime, as wine stewards are few in number and always at their busiest during the evening meal.

Passengers are not normally permitted to bring their own liquor into the dining room or other public areas.

ALASKA
BRIEFING

U.S.A.

Introduction

When one of the many Texans working on the Trans-Alaska Pipeline gets too uppity, he will be told by a local: "If you're not careful, we'll divide Alaska into two halves and then Texas will be the *third* largest state in the Union."

Yes, Alaska is that big, two and a half times the size of Texas; 586,400 square miles of it. And it runs through *four* time zones—Pacific, Yukon, Alaska and Bering, almost to the International Dateline.

And the country is as varied as its size. It's by no means all Eskimos and polar bears, snow and glaciers—though there are 100,000 of the latter. The *south-eastern Panhandle,* from Ketchikan via Juneau up to Haines and Skagway, has a moderate climate, plentiful rain, a green and fertile land, with considerable forests. The *Gulf Coast,* north and west of

Haines around the Gulf of Alaska, is the most densely populated, centering on Anchorage, the state's only real metropolis, the social hub of Alaska, especially since the oil boom. But just north-east of Anchorage is the experimental agricultural area of Matanuska Valley where they grow cabbages bigger than you can get your arms around.

The *Western* region, including the Alaskan Peninsula and the Aleutian and Pribilof Is-lands, is foggy, wet and windy, great for sea- and bird-life but tough on people who don't like wet and windy wilderness. The *Interior* south of the Brooks Range from the Canadian Yukon border towards the Bering Sea has a dry climate, a land of extremes, hot as Arizona in summer, cold as Alaska in winter. The midnight sun makes it possible to play all-night baseball in Fairbanks on June 21, without floodlights. And the *Arctic*,

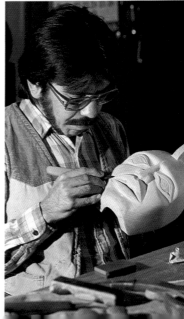

44

extending from Kotzebue above the Seward Peninsula in the west around Barrow to the North Slope at Prudhoe Bay—this is the bleak wasteland of permanently frozen soil (permafrost), temperatures ranging from a July high of 40° F to a January *average* of –17° F, of the popular imagination. And the bankers', for this is where they found the oil.

The population profiting from the state's new-found prosperity numbers around 400,000 (fluctuating with flow of transient labour), half of the people living in Anchorage. The population has doubled since 1960 in the wake of the oil-drilling and laying of the Trans-Alaska Pipeline. The white Americans have come principally from the western states, many with oil-industry experience from Texas, but also from all those areas of the U.S. where the taste for wide open spaces could no longer be satisfied. A certain frontier spirit still exists among these "new pioneers".

The 55,000-strong "native peoples" have made their presence increasingly felt in recent years. In a rare act of unity, the Eskimos, Aleuts and Indians together pressured the U.S. Congress into approving in 1971 a favourable Alaska Native Land Claims Settlement Act which gave them 40 million acres of land and nearly a billion dollars. It was not too much to be done for people previously denied their heritage after inhabiting the place for at least the past 15,000 years.

Anthropologists agree that Eskimos, Aleuts and Indians all are of Asian origin, having crossed into North America over the Bering Sea land bridge that once linked the two continents. The first to cross the "bridge"—in pursuit of migrating mammals seeking new grazing-lands—were the Indians. Some, the Tlingit, Haida and Tsimshian, settled on the bountiful Pacific coast, while the Athabascans moved into the grim, demanding territories of the interior. The Aleuts made their way down to the equally harsh environment of the archipelago that bears their name, the Aleutian Islands. The Eskimos, who share a common ancestry with the Aleuts and are today the most numerous of the three groups, spread along the Arctic coast. Today, these peoples continue to inhabit the territories settled by their forefathers, though considerably diminished in numbers.

A Brief History

40,000–15,000 B.C.	The settlement of the American continent begins with hunters from Siberia crossing the now submerged Bering Sea land bridge into Alaska.
18th century	Czar Peter the Great sends Danish sailor Vitus Bering on first expedition in 1725 to explore North Pacific and investigate stories of a habitable land mass east of Siberia. Sights and names Saint Lawrence Island southwest of Seward peninsula, in 1728. New expedition of 1741 sights Alaskan mainland. Russians begin hunting sea otter with Aleuts press-ganged for fur trade. Alexander Baranov sets up a fur-trading post at Sitka in 1799 where he is named manager of Russian-American Company.
19th century	In 1819 a census numbers the Russian colony as 391 Russians, 22 Creoles and 8,384 Natives, (an estimated 50,000 more natives live outside Russian jurisdiction). Czar Alexander II approaches U.S. to sell them Alaska, but talks are suspended because of American Civil War. In 1867 U.S. Secretary of State William H. Seward negotiates purchase for $7,200,000, which ultimately works out at two cents an acre. Gold is discovered on Gastineau Channel by Richard Harris and Joseph Juneau in 1880, after whom the future state capital is named, nearby the paydirt. First U.S. Alaska census counts 33,416 Natives and 2,045 Whites.
20th century	First territorial legislature, with women voting in Alaska before they get the vote in the U.S. (and two years before Alaskan Natives get the vote) in 1913. First bill for Alaskan statehood is presented to Congress in 1916. U.S. Depression brings farmers in 1930's from Midwest to Alaska. In 1935, Matanuska Valley agricultural project starts north-east of Anchorage with New Deal funds.
	The last important Alaskan gold mine is shut down at Juneau in 1944 to release labour force for war effort. January 3, 1959, Alaska proclaimed 49th state of the

Union. Oil is pumped for first time on North Slope, at Prudhoe Bay in 1968. Plans are made to build the Trans-Alaska Pipeline and construction begins at Prudhoe Bay in 1974. The next year, the state's gross product increases to nearly $6,000,000,000, double that of the year prior to start of the pipeline. Alaska voters choose Willow, near Anchorage, in 1976 as site to replace Juneau as state capital, but prohibitive costs postpone the move. Trans-Alaska Pipeline is completed at Valdez in 1977 and first oil shipped down to the "lower 48" at Puget Sound.

Shopping

It would be silly to buy in Alaska what you can find almost anywhere else in the United States, but there are some items, especially **clothing,** that, despite the generally higher cost of living here, are better bargains than in the "lower 48".

Clearly, Alaskans know best how to dress for the winter, so forget your summer holiday a moment and think ahead. Look out for the padded and often fur-trimmed **parka,** a word the Russian traders borrowed from Siberia for this distinctively Eskimo jacket with its ruff and attached hood. Another Eskimo innovation for the winter are the **mukluks,** soft fur-lined leather or sheepskin bootees that make terrific slippers after a day in the snow. You'll also find first-class **gloves** and other leather and knitwear, often with Indian totemic crests.

The most luxurious items of local knitwear are the **scarves, capes** and **sweaters** made from *qiviut* (pronounced "key-vy-ute"), almost as soft if not quite as fine as cashmere; it is actually the underwool shed by musk-oxen in the spring.

If this clothing has been made by native craftsmen, it will bear the "Silver Hand" emblem as a guarantee of authenticity, i.e. that the craftsman is at least a quarter Eskimo, Aleut or Indian.

One of the prized objects of native craftwork is the delicate **Aleut basket** woven from the wild beach rye grass of the Aleutian Islands shredded by the weaver's fingernails until it is as fine as silk.

The best of the locally made **jewellery** is of jade or ivory (the soapstone is imported, though locally carved). **Scrimshaw ivory,** etched from whale teeth or walrus tusks and coloured by natural dyes, makes some excellent rings, bracelets, earrings and necklace-pendants (and **cribbage-boards**). **Jade** is a relatively new craft in Alaska though the stuff has been lying around for centuries in the Arctic region of the Kobuk River. Much of what you might find in Juneau or other Panhandle towns may well have been carved from pieces still being hacked from a huge slab left standing up in Kotzebue, where it had been ordered (but never collected) by Argentine dictator Juan Peron to make a statue of his wife Eva.

Also popular as a souvenir

is the **gold nugget jewellery,** genuine enough gold and sometimes attractive, but more often looking like somebody's lost tooth-filling or a piece of gilded popcorn.

Eating Out

First choice when eating out in Alaska is not hard: go for the **fish.** (It's fresh, while steaks most often are deep-frozen.) The **Pacific salmon** deserves your attention, especially the **Chinook,** and the **king crab, red snapper, halibut, scallops** and **shrimp,** too, as long as you insist that they be prepared simply—grilled, baked, sautéed or steamed. It would be a shame to spoil them with some dubious "French" sauce.

This being a frontier society, the best meals are often the heartiest stomach-fillers. The spicy **gumbo soups** and **stews**—a Creole dish with okra and rice and chicken, ham or shrimp—were evidently brought up here by Louisiana oilmen. In Juneau, you can get a 24-hour hunger-stilling **poorboy sandwich,** on a loaf half as long as a French baguette and stuffed with every sausage, ham, cheese, pickle and salad that the "cook" can get his hands on.

Practical Information

Banks and currency exchange: Open 8.30 a.m. to 3 p.m., Monday to Thursday (later on Fridays). Currency exchange in major hotels and at Juneau Airport.

Post Offices: Open 8 a.m. to 5 p.m., Monday to Friday, in some places till 6 p.m. on Fridays. Mail from Alaska is very slow, even by airmail you must add a week or two to the time it would take from the "lower 48". For quick communications, use Western Union for telegrams or for sending money-orders.

Shopping Hours: 9 or 9.30 a.m. to 6 p.m., except shopping centres, which stay open much later. Restaurants usually open all day.

BRITISH COLUMBIA
BRIEFING

Canada

Introduction

"Such a land", said Rudyard Kipling in 1908, "is good for an energetic man. It is also not bad for a loafer." That's still true today.

British Columbia is supremely the land of the wild outdoors, with the constant challenge of rugged mountains, dense forests, a jagged coastline and dizzily fast-moving rivers. But its capital is the smiling, sleepy town of Victoria, evoking a genteel British past that even the British themselves may well have forgotten. And the province's principal city, with a population of over a million, is the beautifully situated Vancouver, home of easy good living, sophisticated architecture and all the colour and movement of a major Pacific port. Loafers love it.

Although only third in size among Canada's ten provinces (Quebec and Ontario precede it), British Columbia covers a huge area, four times the size of Britain and larger than any state in the USA —except Alaska.

British Columbia's geographical position between the Pacific Ocean and the great barrier of the Rocky Mountains links it in many ways more closely to the United States than to the rest of Canada. Vancouver, for instance, seems to have more in common with the fellow port cities of Seattle and even San Francisco than it does with Calgary, principal city of neighbouring Alberta.

The province's population (over 2,700,000) is predominantly British—with a particularly large Scottish contingent, the territory having originally been named New Caledonia. The rest are mainly of German, French, Dutch, Ukrainian, Italian or Scandinavian origin. Vancouver— sharing another feature more with Seattle or San Francisco than with neighbouring Canadian towns—has large Chinese and Japanese communities. Native Indians, who outnumbered Europeans three-to-one 100 years ago, now number 55,000.

The vigorous mix of people in B.C., as it is familiarly called, nearly all crowd into the south-western corner of the province, around Vancouver, some three-quarters of the population packed happily into only 5 per cent of their vast territory.

Perversely attached to the climate of their mother country, the British immigrants seem very much at home in the frequent rainfalls of the coastal region, though it must be added that the warm Japanese Pacific current takes the bite off the winters. On balance, the climate of British Columbia is generally milder than that of the British Isles.

It certainly makes for a green and pleasant land, with Victoria's magnificent Butchart Gardens offering a concentration of the province's riches in flowers and trees. Trees are of course a major source of B.C.'s economic prosperity. The spruce, fir and cedar provide three-quarters of Canada's lumber and considerable quantities of woodpulp and paper. Vancouver Island, 280 miles long, is covered by the largest stand of lumber in the world.

B.C. had its gold rush, too, back in 1858, but its important mining reserves today are centred on the rather more mundane lead, zinc, copper and aluminium.

The other great natural resource is the fish of the Pacific coast and the Fraser and Columbia rivers. Energetic fishermen and loafing gourmets alike appreciate B.C.'s salmon and trout. You will, too.

A Brief History

16th–18th centuries	Sir Francis Drake, English navigator, sails up to Vancouver Island and along the coast of British Columbia in 1579, after stopping off near San Francisco during his voyage around the world.

Juan Perez, sent north from Mexico by the Spanish in 1774, reaches Queen Charlotte Islands, trades with Indians. Captain Cook lands at Nootka Sound on Vancouver Island before going off to Hawaii. British and American traders follow in 1780's to start fur trade with Indians.

British force Spanish to abandon their exclusive claim to the territory and Captain George Vancouver, a member of Cook's expeditions, is sent out to take formal possession. In 1793 Alexander Mackenzie completes first overland crossing of North American continent, arriving on B.C.'s Pacific coast at Bella Coola inlet.

19th century	Between 1805 and 1849 trading posts are set up by North West Company (Nor'-Westers) led by Simon Fraser, explorer of legendary intrepidity, especially as rider of rapids. Territory along north Pacific coast is parcelled out between Americans and British, and 49th parallel established as boundary from the Rocky Mountains to the Pacific Ocean. Vancouver Island becomes a Crown Colony in 1849. Gold is discovered up the Fraser River in the spring of 1858. By the summer, to head off any American designs on it, the mainland territory is made a new British colony. Hitherto named New Caledonia by the predominantly Scottish Nor'-Westers and Hudson's Bay Company traders, it becomes British Columbia, Queen Victoria's personal choice. November 19th, James Douglas, former head of Hudson's Bay Company's west coast operations, is proclaimed first Governor.

British Columbia agrees in 1871 to join with Vancouver Island as one province in the Dominion of Canada on the understanding that Canadian Pacific Railroad will reach B.C. in the next decade. Delays bring serious threat of secession in 1876, but population increases rapidly and by the 1880's the whites for the first time overtake the Indians (then 25,000).

20th century	Trade is given spectacular boost in 1915 by building of Panama Canal to open up fast access to European markets. Indians are given vote for the first time in provincial elections in 1949. In the 1950's, the Rocky Mountain barrier is breached by Trans-Mountain oil-pipeline from Edmonton, Alberta, and the Trans-Canadian Highway.

Shopping

Shopping on holiday is of course a quest for something out of the ordinary. The shops of Victoria and Vancouver are well stocked with international fashions and luxury goods that are now exported all over the world. But British Columbia has something more distinctive to offer: the products of its native Indians. These are to be found in specialist craft shops, native art galleries and museum gift-

shops and in the craft areas of large department stores.

The most beautiful work particular to this region of North America is the gleaming black **argillite carving** of the Haida Indians from the islands of B.C.'s Pacific coast. The slate-like rock is hewn principally from Slatechuck Mountain on the Queen Charlotte Islands and is used for small-scale versions of the tribe's intricately carved **totem poles.** Yes, you can buy

an authentic totem pole, but even a small one will set you back $5,000 so you might prefer one of the exquisite pendants or other jewellery bearing ornate tribal family crests, for a fraction of that.

The Haida have also applied their craftsmanship to **gold bracelets,** highly prized by connoisseurs.

Further down the price scale are the brightly painted **wood carvings** of the Kwakiutl Indians, and **silkscreen** designs of the thunderbird emblem that make splendid greetings cards.

The Coast Salish Indians are specialists in wool-weaving, still doing all the washing, carding and spinning by hand, with natural dyes from lichen, flowers and roots. They weave the multi-coloured patterns of mountain scenery, animals and birds into small **rugs** or **wall-hangings.** From Nootka comes the surprisingly sturdy basketware made from the wild sweet grass of Vancouver Island's west coast.

The authenticity of such craftwork is guaranteed by a Department of Indian Affairs label with the emblem of a sprawling beaver pelt.

One of the most sought-after "cottage industry" items is the hand-knitted **Cowichan sweater.** In fact, these handsome, durable and waterproof woollens are a rare and delightful example of collaboration between Indians and settlers. The Cowichan knit the sweaters with eagle or whale motifs in their homes in the time-honoured seamless style taught them by Scottish settlers in the 19th century.

Chinatown, principally in Vancouver but also in Victoria, is also a great source of unusual gifts. From Hong Kong, Taiwan and mainland China, look out for **Chinese** statuary, porcelain, cooking implements, bamboo baskets and hats, incense, jade and carved wood. Lacquered pottery is of especially high quality and there are excellent bargains in quilted jackets—a good idea if you're on your way to Alaska—embroidered dresses and silk and satin blouses.

From the Chinese grocery stores there are well-packed food delicacies; try taking home a bag of fortune cookies.

Eating Out

If you get the chance to lunch or dine in British Columbia, be sure to try the local seafood. Gourmets the world over acknowledge the superiority of B.C.'s Pacific salmon. There are six principal local varieties—sockeye, coho, pink, chum, spring and steelhead, in descending order of delicacy. Sockeye and coho grilled and served with a lemon butter sauce are a royal meal. The salmon is also superb smoked (with a good glass of Norwegian akvavit or Polish vodka). They'll even pack a whole smoked salmon for you and mail it home for Christmas—or even sooner.

But the Pacific shores also bring marvellous red snapper, halibut, crab, shrimp, scallops, mussels, abalone and from inland waterways come some fine rainbow trout. The salmon can also be superb. Around Vancouver Island, they make a mean clam chowder soup, adding onions, potatoes and cream to the clams. The locals and not a few New Englanders compare it favourably to Boston's famous concoction.

Chinese Food

Thanks once more to Chinatown, B.C.'s Chinese cuisine is among the best on the American continent. One of the delights of the traditional *Peking* and *Cantonese* restaurants is the "dim sum" trolley which is rolled past your table with an array of pork or shrimp wrapped in rice pastry, spare ribs in black bean sauce, steamed tripe or chicken feet, or an egg custard dessert. Other regions have now added their cuisines, including a sophisticated range of *Szechuan*, rich and spicy, ideal on a cold night—try the soups, the hot Szechuan shrimp or the whole stewed duck; *Hunan*, more delicate, with subtle uses of honey and ginger in hams and

chicken; and *Shanghai*, sister port-city, excellent for seeing what the Chinese can do with B.C.'s seafood—try the abalone braised in a sesame sauce.

Tea

And then there's tea-time, the hallowed moment that put the "British" into British Columbia. In Victoria, the ritual is performed with a loving care that will bring a tear to every Anglophile's eye. You'll find the very best varieties of tea—rich Darjeeling, perfumed Earl Grey, smoky Lapsang Suchong and down-to-earth nice cuppa Ceylon and Orange Pekoe. The elegant pots are correctly scalded, the brew properly steeped, and poured to your liking *before* or *after* adding milk—two schools of thought that have never really established who's right. The tea is served with dainty little sandwiches, muffins, pastries and scones —which American Southerners understandably confuse with their "biscuits" though a Scotsman will set them straight on the proper consistency of the dough. (The biscuits served in Victoria are of course "cookies" south of the border.) A further note: "one lump or two?" is an offer of sugar, not cream.

Practical Information

Banks and currency exchange: 10 a.m. to 3 p.m., Monday to Thursday (later on Fridays). Currency exchange in major hotels.

Credit cards and traveller's cheques: All the major cards and traveller's cheques are accepted. You'll need your passport or driver's licence for traveller's cheques.

Currency: The Canadian dollar fluctuates at around 20 per cent less than the U.S. dollar. The latter is accepted in most establishments at a rate only one or two per cent less favourable than at the bank, so unless you're intending to make a major purchase, you may not want to make the exchange from U.S. to Canadian dollars. Pennies (1), nickels (5), dimes (10), quarters (25 cents) and dollar bills (banknotes) are similar to the U.S. versions but not identical, so don't use the wrong ones in automats.

National or regional holidays (in spring and summer): Victoria Day, Monday preceding May 25; Canada Day, July 1; British Columbia Day, first Monday in August; Labour Day, first Monday in September. (Most shops and all banks and public buildings are closed on these days and Sundays.)

Police: Friendly and efficient as well as legendary, the Royal Canadian Mounted Police are located in Vancouver at 1200 West 73rd Avenue (phone 732-4511); Victoria at 775 Topaz Avenue (388-3668); Prince Rupert at 100 West Sixth Avenue (624-2136).

Post Offices: Open 8 a.m. to 5.45 p.m., Monday to Friday, 9 a.m. to 12 noon on Saturdays. (Vancouver: West Georgia Street; Victoria: Federal Building; Prince Rupert: West 2nd Avenue.)

Restaurants: Though fast-food chains and smarter restaurants close a little later, lunch is generally served from 11 a.m. to 2 p.m., dinner from 6 p.m. to 11 p.m. Tipping is rarely included in the bill—15% is normal.

Shops: 9 a.m. to 6 p.m. Monday to Saturday, later on Thursdays and Fridays in some department stores and shopping centres.

THE GLACIERS
OF ALASKA

Introduction

Before you've seen one, you could be excused for thinking that a glacier was nothing but an overgrown, frozen river. But your trip to Alaska will take you right up close to several of these marvellous monsters. There, you'll be able to see that the impact of the freezing of the snows into glacial ice and the ponderous, inexorable movement down from the mountains to the valley or the sea below have created a phenomenon that is totally, awe-inspiringly unique.

These glaciers, remember, have been moving—advancing, retreating, advancing again—for the past 12½ million years. Columbia Bay, Glacier Bay, the Mendenhall Glacier at Juneau, the Taku Glacier and dozens of others, massive or minuscule, up and down the coast offer a direct visible link to that eery moment in the earth's evolution that Alaska today still seems to represent in the popular imagination: the Ice Age.

Looking at them, you suddenly realize how woefully inadequate a valiant dictionary definition can be. The venerable Oxford suggests: "An immense mass or river of ice in a high mountain valley, formed by the descent and consolidation of the snow that falls on the higher ground." True. But that doesn't even begin to suggest the fantastic complexity contained in the dynamic concept of the glacier. This frozen mass is in a perpetual state of change, flux, growth, disintegration and recuperation, subject to the vagaries of temperature, snowfall and the other geological processes going on around and under it. They are, in fact, in a strange sort of a way, "alive"...

There are Glaciers and Glaciers

The experts tell us we can't just talk about "a glacier". There are several different types of glacial formation and glacierologists have a specific language to describe them.

First of all, there is the *alpine glacier* found high in the mountains, with a smaller version known as a *cirque*, shaped like a somewhat elongated amphitheatre.

Ice caps are high-altitude glacial flows filling a large basin or plateau. When the ice cap spills over the edge, it

forms the classical glacier that most people think of, the *valley glacier,* cutting out its U-shaped channel through the downhill terrain.

When two valley glaciers join each other at the foot of the mountains and flow on as one, they form a fan-shaped *piedmont glacier.*

Several high-altitude glaciers flowing together, separated only by mountain tops and ridges, form a vast *ice field,* the best known in Alaska

You cannot fail to be overawed by a glacier's sheer grandeur.

being the Juneau Icefield. Finally, there is an even more immense glacial formation covering a whole land mass, the *ice sheet* or *continental glacier* found in Antarctica and Greenland. Ice sheets disappeared from Alaska 10 to 15,000 years ago.

Glaciers on the Go

Glaciers are moving all the time, but some are advancing and others, while their ice mass is still moving forward, are retreating. When the accumulation of ice is greater than the amount that is melting, the glacier is *advancing*. The glacierologists call it a "healthy" glacier. The Johns Hopkins at Glacier Bay and the Taku near Juneau are very healthy. When the ice is melting faster than the glacier can accumulate ice to replace it, it's *retreating*. It's "sick". The Columbia and the Mendenhall are sick. (As residents around Lake Mendenhall will tell you, the "sickness" can be benign—it leaves more space for a garden.)

The glacier's movement is of course imperceptible to anyone just standing there watching. But modern technology such as the Doppler laser system, airborne radar

and space satellite photography permits very accurate measurement of the glacier's rate of progress.

The Taku is advancing a few hundred feet per year, the Mendenhall retreating at about 90 feet per year. But sometimes glaciers move really "fast", making what the experts call a short-lived *surge*. For instance, the Black Rapids Glacier in the Alaska Range was nicknamed the "Galloping Glacier" in 1937 for surging more than three miles in six months, threatening the Richardson Highway between Valdez and Fairbanks. Although it is at present retreating, the experts fear it may be getting ready for another gallop.

"In the Summer, When it Sizzles..."

So just what *is* this stuff that crawls, surges or gallops across the Alaskan landscape? Alaska geologist Bruce Molna says, in his dry geological way, that it's "a perennial accumulation of ice, snow, water, rock and sediment that moves under the influence of gravity." Aha! There's more to it than just a river of ice.

But to begin with, it's not just ordinary ice, it's specifically *glacial ice,* created by years of snowfalls freezing one on top of another building up enormous pressure. The pressure freezes the snowflakes first into granular ice or *firn* and finally the bubbly glacial ice, the blue stuff that you'll see as you cruise up to Glacier Bay or Columbia.

GLACIERS

Why is it blue? Because blue is the only colour not absorbed by the physical characteristics of the water molecules in the ice. This effect is heightened on days without sun. (Some of it is also a dirty brown, but that's the sediment that we'll get to later.)

And bubbly? Pockets of air trapped inside the glacial ice create a phenomenon called *ice sizzle*. As the ice melts or moves along, the bubbles burst, several simultaneously, and you can hear the glacier's interior snap, crackle and pop. In icebergs shed or *calved* by the glacier into the sea, the ice sizzle is sometimes quite violent, causing the iceberg suddenly to keel over.

As that mass of ice moves downhill, it not only sizzles, it also cracks wide open at times into *crevasses* as it drops down uneven terrain or is subjected to sudden changes in temperature. The crevasses can be treacherous for anyone venturing out onto the ice as they drop 100 to 150 feet inside the body of ice.

The glacier surface develops wave-like *ogives*, curving ribs that resemble the ripples in chocolate icing on a cake, as the glacier surface progresses faster than the ice lower down. (The base is anything from a

Bourbon on the Rocks

"Ice sizzle" can have hazardous effects in the most peaceful situations. Glacierologists working in Alaska drilled down through one of their thickest glaciers to a depth of 2,000 feet. To celebrate the successful operation, they opened a bottle of whisky and brought some of the glacier ice up to serve as cubes to chill their drinks. One after another, the whisky glasses exploded as the cubes developed "ice sizzle" under the impact of the alien fluid.

few hundred to 2,000 feet deep.) The texture of the ice is also affected by streams of water running on top, inside or underneath the glacier, melting it as they go.

So much for the ice, but the rock and sediment are integral parts of the glacier, too. The glacier is a formidable factor in land erosion, scraping along particles of rock known as *rock flour*. When it picks up larger rocks, the action is described as *plucking*. It is the valley glaciers' U-shaped erosion extending into the sea that creates the inlets we call *fjords*.

The rock and sediment thrown up by the glacier's advance creates a moraine—*lateral moraine* at the edges or banks of the glacier, and sometimes a *medial moraine* down the middle where two glaciers have flowed together from adjoining valleys to form a piedmont.

The moraine left by a retreating glacier at its terminus has a very varied terrain. It is often pocked by deep hollows or *kettles* created by embedded blocks of ice left behind by the receding glacier and subsequently melted. The kettles often fill with water to form ponds. Sediment that has built up in the crevasses is left in long meandering hardened ridges or *eskers* when the glacier retreats.

Alive and Well and Living on a Glacier

Terminal moraines have a distinctive flora. Indeed, a glacier has its own ecosystem. There are creatures that choose deliberately to live on and in the glacier. The *ice worm* is three quarters of an inch long, with the diameter of a darning needle. A close cousin of the earthworm, it thrives in temperatures just above freezing. When the sun comes out, it wiggles below the surface of the glacier to get out of the heat. It lives off red algae.

Sharing the algae is the *snow flea,* though he prefers conifer pollen.

The plant life that appears first on the bare rock of the exposed moraine is the *lichen,* a compound plant of algae and fungus. Its presence is vital to the study of the glacier's activity and past history, since the lichen's growth at a constant rate can be accurately measured to determine the rate of a glacier's retreat.

You'll also see bright patches of *moss* and the pretty red-flowered *fireweed.*

One creature which does not live on the glacier but depends on it to a certain extent for the survival of the species is the *seal.* When the glacier calves its icebergs or floes into the sea, they provide a safe haven for pregnant mother seals to perch on while they do some calving of their own, safe from the attacks of predators on dry land. Seals abound in various spots such as in Prince William Sound

near the terminus of the Columbia Glacier.

They may be perched on a relic of their Ice Age ancestors. The glaciers are full of fossilized skulls, teeth, bones and whole limbs of mammoths, mastodons, sabretooth tigers, lions and yaks. Recently, the foot of a prehistoric bison was thrown up by a glacier near Fairbanks.

Many of the Ice Age relics first came to light in the glacier silt-deposits dug up by gold miners at the end of the last century. It was not uncommon for prospectors to be trailed by paleontologists hoping to find their own treasures in the debris discarded by the gold miners. One of them was a young German immigrant named Otto Geist hired by Childs Frick, scion of the wealthy industrialist family, to pick the fossils out of the miners' jetsam. They're now on display in the New York Museum of Natural History.

PORTS OF CALL

SEATTLE

U.S.A.

Introduction

Bright and energetic, Seattle is blessed with one of those natural locations that render public relations superfluous. Its bay on Puget Sound is surrounded by the green, green country of Washington state with the snow-capped Olympic and Cascade mountains looming in the background, and Mount Rainier towering over them all. The climate is fresh and moist enough to earn the town its sobriquet of the "Emerald City".

In town, Pioneer Square, dating from the last century, and traditional waterside markets lie side by side with contemporary architecture. The Seattle Center, with its distinctive Space Needle built for the 1962 World's Fair, offers magnificent views of the city and surrounding scenery. On a clear day, and given good eyesight, it is possible to see Mount St. Helen's, which erupted in March 1980, about 165 miles (265 km.) south of the city.

Few traces remain of the city's colourful, if rough, beginnings in the 1850s. The superb natural outer harbour, Elliott Bay, was ideal for the transport of timber brought down from the vast forests of the Northwest, as well as the import of luxuries from the Orient. Seattle was also the springboard for the Alaska and Klondike gold rushes of the 1880s and 1890s. Although the timber industry still thrives in Seattle, the town's present-day prosperity is linked more strongly with that of the aeronautical industry—Boeing has a plant based just outside the city.

The region holds many attractions; the nearby mountains offer top-class skiing, climbing and hiking, and relaxation is all too easy in and around the countless lakes dotted with boats ranging in size from tiny dinghies to majestic yachts.

A Brief History

19th century   The first settlement is established on the western shore of Elliott Bay at Alki Point in 1851. Two years later, the expanding sawmill town is planned and laid out, named Seattle after the friendly Suquamish Indian chief Seathl. Successive disasters—an Indian raid in 1856, anti-

Chinese riots in the 1880s, the fire of 1889—hinder development until the railroad arrives in 1893. Seattle takes advantage of the Alaskan gold rush and growing trade with the Far East to forge its own prosperity.

1900–1960   Expansion continues, but at a slower pace. The Panama Canal (1914) encourages more shipping to the U.S. East Coast and Europe. The Lake Washington Canal, built in 1916, creates a route from inner to outer harbour. Seattle's fortunes are hard hit by the Great Depression of the 1930s. The switch to a wartime economy mobilizes natural resources and industrial capacity. Shipyards serve the war in the Pacific, and the new aircraft industry gains a foothold. Business slumps again during the 1950s.

1961–present day   Seattle draws the world's attention to its progress and potential by holding an International World's·Fair in 1962. The city is now a major centre on the Pacific coast for forestry and air- and spacecraft, for the financial world, and for futuristic electronics and biomedical industries.

Sightseeing

The attractions of cosmopolitan Seattle are immensely varied, catering to every taste, whether for art and music, sightseeing, shopping or dining out at one of many fine restaurants. Although you can choose to take a taxi, bus or monorail, most of the city centre can be reached on foot from the large hotels. This way it is easier to get the feel of Seattle and to begin to see why, increasingly, people are finding it so desirable a place in which to live.

Pioneer Square (First Avenue and Yeslerway) is the only vestige of the good old days. Its Victorian red-brick has been spared the urban developers' wrecking ball, and the pleasant tree-shaded little square is surrounded by some good restaurants (both expensive and modest), quality boutiques and excellent jazz clubs. Look out for the ornate pergola, in fact a bus shelter.

You can explore Seattle's lower depths on an **Underground Tour** (from 610 First Avenue). It leads you through the subterranean city that was burned out in 1889 and buried under today's sidewalks, streets and buildings, which were simply erected on top. You'll see old shops and façades and eerie galleries, enlivened by the guide's amusing stories of the town's beginnings.

The **International District,** bounded by Fourth and Eighth avenues and Main and Lane streets, includes Chinatown and the Japanese neighbourhood. You'll find dozens of jade and jewellery shops here, great restaurants, a Buddhist temple and the **Wing Luke Memorial Museum** (414 Eighth Street) which traces the intriguing history of Chinese immigration to the West Coast during the mining and railway construction days of the 19th century.

Sport is very much a part of Seattle's present, and the nearby **Kingdome** is home to major league baseball, football, basketball and soccer teams. It can also accommodate industrial and trade fairs and is open to the public for guided tours.

Sooner or later, everyone comes to **Pike Place Market,** with its extravagant displays of fruit and vegetables, fish and flowers. Although these stalls, which spill over on two levels, attract visitors from round the world, Pike Place is a working market which keeps locals supplied with a cornucopia of fresh foods. Small shops, like Italian delicatessens or Chinese groceries—so atmospheric they transport you thousands of miles as you go through the door—stock the essentials for a multitude of national cuisines.

The great symbol of Seattle is the 607-foot (185-m.) **Space Needle** standing on a tripod, a proud relic of the 1962 World's Fair that gave Seattle a much-needed boost after its 1950s' slump. There is a revolving restaurant and an observatory at the top from which you have a splendid **view** across the city to the Olympic and Cascade mountain ranges dominated by Mount Rainier.

Immediately below the Needle is the **Seattle Center,** which also grew out of the World's Fair. It groups the Opera House, Playhouse, Coliseum and several museums. The **Pacific Science Center** is a spectacular structure designed by Minoru Yamasaki to house exhibits on space exploration, laser technology, and above all, the oceanography of Puget Sound. Under the same roof are the **Museum of Flight,** and the **Northwest Craft Center and Gallery** with exhibitions featuring the Indian cultures of the Pacific Northwest. The **Art Museum Pavilion** (a branch of the Seattle Art Museum in Volunteer Park, known for its excellent Asian collection) features contemporary American and regional artists, as well as major travelling exhibitions.

The university **arboretum,** further out towards Lake Washington, is a haven for travellers and gardening enthusiasts alike. Even the most ardent horticulturalist may not be able to identify all 5,000 species of trees and plants brought here from around the world, but no one can fail to appreciate their beauty, or the contemplative serenity of the Japanese Garden. The **Woodland Zoological Gardens** may not be as peaceful, but the zoo itself is superb and justly popular.

Like any self-respecting port, Seattle is liveliest along the **waterfront**. More than 90 piers stretch some 50 miles (80 km.) along the shores of Elliott Bay, which gives access out to the Pacific. A drive along the Alaskan Way follows the sweeping coastline northwards, but the panoramic route on the Alaskan Way viaduct high above sea-level pays extra dividends, with the splendours of Puget Sound and the snow-capped mountains unfolding in the distance.

Pier 90 combines business with pleasure. Its wharves were once piled high with tea and timber, and work still goes on along the quayside, where ships from all over the world are berthed. Further along, the Gold Rush Strip at Piers 50–59 celebrates wild, exhilarating days. There is still treasure to be found in the shops here. Life at the depths is brought up to eye level at the **Aquarium** (Pier 59). Stop by to feast your eyes on octopus, sharks, eels, seals and salmon, or watch a film on the watery depths in the Omnidome theatre.

Excursions

Any visit to the waterfront should include a **boat ride.** From Pier 56, harbour tours on board the *Goodtime* offer a new perspective on Seattle's skyline and its incomparable setting among the natural wonders of the Olympic Peninsula and the Cascade Range. From the ferry terminal on Pier 52 you can take a 35-minute trip to Bainbridge Island, for a walk around the quaint town of Winslow. The British Columbia Steamship Company operates the *Princess Margaret* to Victoria, B.C., a four-hour trip (Pier 69). There is also a hydrofoil excursion daily to Vancouver.

An expedition to **Sultan,** 39 miles (63 km.) west of the city, will transport you back to the days of the gold rush in an authentically restored town. If you prefer something more contemporary, the new **winery** at Chateau Ste. Michelle, 15 miles (24 km.) north-east of Seattle, offers tours through its ultra-modern wine-making facility, as well as a chance to sample wine made from grapes grown in the Yakima Valley.

If you prefer the untamed wilds of the American Northwest, you have only to decide which way to turn. The ravaged beauty of **Mount St. Helen's** lies only 90 miles (145 km.) from Seattle. You can survey the devastated coun-

tryside from one of two "interpretative centers" within the Gifford Pinchot National Park, as well as studying the volcano in safety, with the help of videos and photographs.

If the silhouette of Mount Rainier has proved too inviting to resist, take an excursion out to the **Mount Rainier National Park**, two hours south of town, for some exhilarating hiking on its rugged slopes. Here, too, the mountains are volcanic, but so far inactive. Further down the slopes, subalpine forests are ablaze from late spring with an amazing profusion of delicate wild flowers.

To the north-east is the equally staggering **Cascade National Park,** with glaciers, forest and lakes. But, if you think you've run out of superlatives, a trip to the **Olympic Peninsula** and its Olympic National Forest and National Park are in order—900,000

acres (364,000 ha.) of untouched wilderness to be sampled on short walks from the car, on hikes into the interior, by canoe or on horseback.

Not surprisingly, the city is also famous for its sports clothing and equipment for mountaineering, fishing and hunting.

Shopping

The only difficulty of shopping in Seattle is one of choice—department store, exquisite boutique or waterfront stall. There are hand-made lace blouses, the latest *haute couture*, and designer baby clothes. Many stores sell china, sculpture and pottery, paintings and artefacts.

Indian and Eskimo art, both traditional and modern, is sold in galleries, on waterfront piers and in specialist shops in Pioneer Square.

Eating Out

Seattle's restaurants reflect the city's cosmopolitan image. Naturally, seafood holds pride of place—what could surpass freshly boiled Dungeness crab from a waterfront fish bar? Every chef has a speciality of the day featuring oysters, clams or Pacific salmon. European cuisines are well represented, but a meal in one of the many fine Chinese, Japanese or Polynesian restaurants can truly transport you to unimagined shores.

VICTORIA

Canada

Introduction

Probably the most genteel city in all of North America, Victoria is a town of another age, another world. Flowers everywhere. Geraniums in the baskets hanging from the five-bulb lamp-posts in the city's shopping streets. Hydrangeas and roses in the lovingly tended gardens of the residential neighbourhoods, shrubs and more exotic blossoms in the city's parks and conservatories.

In the month of February, while the rest of Canada is still huddling around log-fires and radiators, even just across the Strait of Georgia in Vancouver, the people of Victoria are out in their parks and gardens for the annual flower-count! Yes, they count every blossom in town and the figure regularly tops the 5 million mark. For Victoria is blessed with a mild and sunny climate, with just enough rain to water the flowers, but an annual average (they count everything in this town) of 2,183 hours of sun to give them their brilliant colours. The very air in Victoria is sweet and gentle.

Like Vancouver, it is a port town—at the south-east tip of the forest-covered Vancouver Island. But the port is not so predominantly industrially oriented and thus its harbours, especially the Inner Harbour, are filled with yachts and pleasure-boats, ferries and jolly little seaplanes.

If it weren't for its very-seriously-taken role as British Columbia's legislative capital, Victoria would seem totally conceived for leisure and pleasure. It is indeed a favourite haven for many affluent Canadians to take their retirement, contributing even more to the town's all-pervasive gentility.

But the formidable neo-Romanesque Parliament is there to remind the citizenry of the city's venerable past (all of 140 years) and solemn responsibilities. Characteristically, the Parliament is inspired in its interior by the chamber of London's House of Commons, for here everything seems to have a link to Britain.

Victoria's Britain is the legendary one of fine lawns, discreet manners and all the delicacies surrounding the ritual of tea-time. Taking tea in Victoria appears to be almost more hallowed than it is in the sceptred isle of the mother country. If it emphasizes Victoria's resistance to the rest of the planet's hustle and bustle, so much the better.

A Brief History

16th century	Greek sailor Juan de Fuca in the employ of the Spanish government discovers the strait in 1592 (named after him) immediately to the west of present-day Victoria. Does not go ashore.
19th century	Southern end of Vancouver Island deserted until James Douglas comes looking for a new base for Hudson Bay Company's West Coast operations. Fort Victoria founded 1843. Vancouver Island is made British crown colony with Victoria as its capital in 1848.
	Gold rush up the Fraser River in 1858 turns Victoria into tented city-base for 25,000 prospectors and suppliers. Victoria made capital of new Canadian province of British Columbia, in 1868, two years after Vancouver Island is incorporated with mainland B.C.
1862–1908	The tea served in those days isn't all of the English variety—Victoria is a dope-dealing centre for the miners and there are 14 licenced opium factories in the town till they are closed in 1908.

Sightseeing

The toy-like quality of Victoria is emphasized in its most imposing monumental building, the **Parliament.** Built in 1897, it was certainly erected by someone with a playful sense of what might best evoke merrie olde England. There's a little bit of London's St. Paul's Cathedral in that massive central dome, topped, for want of a saint, by a gilded statue of Captain George Vancouver. The romanesque-arched entrance recalls the British capital's Natural Science Museum and the flanking smaller-domed turrets suggest something between an Englishman's castle and his county council. The whole fantasy effect is enhanced at night when every contour of the Parliament is outlined by thousands of light bulbs. A birthday-child could be forgiven for trying to blow them out.

Inside, you can visit the **debating chamber,** unmistakably modelled on the House of Commons. The great dome's interior, the **rotunda,** is covered with murals painted by

George Southwell to illustrate the four virtues that "made" British Columbia: Courage, as shown by George Vancouver confronting the Spanish at Nootka Sound in 1792; Spirit of Enterprise, James Douglas establishing Fort Victoria for the Hudson's Bay Company in 1842; Work, by those who had to build the Fort; and Justice, meted out to the unruly mob engaged in the 1858 gold rush.

Reasonably enough, the Parliament grounds include a bronze statue of Queen Victoria. It was she who chose the name of British Columbia—rather than New Caledonia, New Hanover, New Cornwall or New Georgia. There is also a **Cenotaph** war monument which is the focus of the annual mid-September Battle of Britain Parade. You can easily get the impression that this town is only nominally in Canada.

Immediately east of the Parliament is the newly housed **Provincial Museum,** devoted to B.C.'s fauna, flora and Indian folklore. In front of the museum is the **Netherlands Carillon Tower,** a 62-bell gift of Dutch-Canadians and biggest bell-tower in the country.

Further east is **Thunderbird Park,** home of the city's most important collection of Indian carvings—not only Tsimshian and Haida totem-poles, but also Salish Coast sculpture of chieftains and a reconstructed Kwakiutl house. The thunderbird, a mythical creature whose eyes flashed the light-

Built over an exhausted limestone quarry, Butchart Gardens provide a fabulous display of vivid colour.

VICTORIA

ning and whose beating wings rumbled the thunder, figures in many of the carvings in the park. There's a **sculpture workshop** where you can see Indians still practicing the ancient skills—with modern tools. The park's wood carvings date for the most part from the last half of the 19th century, but are constantly restored or replaced when weather or worms get the better of them.

At the corner of Dallas Road and Douglas Street is Mile "O" of the 4,860-mile Trans-Canada Highway. It is here that the flowers and greenery of Victoria begin their most delightful assault on you, in **Beacon Hill Park,** 154 acres of gently rolling lawns bordered by flowerbeds, cedars and oaks that stretch down to the Pacific Ocean, to the Strait of Juan de Fuca. Step back from that vast sea for a moment to enjoy the intimacy of the park's

Nessie, Move Over

Victoria has a cousin to the Loch Ness monster, appearing regularly off Vancouver Island's south-east coast. Its name is Caddie, an abbreviation of Cadborosaurus, taking its name from nearby Cadboro Bay where it was first sighted. Eyewitnesses all agree Caddie has a large and hideous head, disturbingly smiling all the time, its extremely long body snaking out behind with three to five humps on it. Sceptics with a knowledgeable scientific bent suggest that it's just an ugly sea-lion followed by three to five of its mates. True believers insist it feeds on ship's barnacles since boats are often lifted suddenly into the air without any other explanation than that Caddie is hungry and is lunching at their expense.

The Mayor of Inverness, Scotland, an expert in the matter of crowd-drawing monsters, in the course of a visit to Victoria expressed the opinion that the fact that he didn't personally see Caddie proved nothing. He'd never seen the Loch Ness monster either, but everybody knew...

Your best chance of seeing Caddie is to stand at Finlayson Point at the end of Beacon Hill Park after drinking your tea with something a little stronger in it than milk.

ponds and the swans imported from England. Look out, too, for the 114-foot totem-pole carved by Chief Mungo Martin and said to be the tallest in existence.

At the northern end of Beacon Hill is the **Crystal Gardens** conservatory. You can have tea there amid tropical plants, exotic birds and lovably repulsive reptiles.

It's right behind the **Empress Hotel,** a place so prestigious and renowned for its elegant servings of tea that it schedules three separate afternoon sittings each day and you're advised to make a reservation if you want to participate in the ritual. Keep your shoes on, but white gloves are optional. At all times, smile. The Empress was built in 1905 to serve passengers ferried across from the western terminus of the Canadian Pacific and is the archetypal grand old railway hotel. As you wade through its carpets, past its wood panelling and brass fittings, the thought might occur that Victoria was named after London's station rather than after England's Queen.

There's rather a good replica of the latter, looking decidedly unamused, in the **Royal London Wax Museum** (on Belleville Street beside the

Inner Harbour) or, if you prefer, a nice and cheerful Charles and Di.

The **Inner Harbour** itself makes a pleasant place to loiter among the yachts and seaplanes. If you like underwater life, try the harbour's **Undersea Gardens.** Besides the usually exquisite tropical specimens, there's a perfectly horrid giant octopus. The Pacific salmon look as gloomy as they taste delicious.

There are two other museums worth your attention. The **Maritime Museum,** which now occupies the old courthouse on Bastion Square, contains some neat models and navigational paraphernalia of the merchant ships of yore, whalers, steamers and the old Hudson's Bay paddle-wheelers. The star attraction is the orginal *Tilikum,* a 38-foot dugout canoe that was equipped with three sails to take Captain J.C. Voss in 1901 on a crazy 40,000-mile three-year voyage around the world. He sailed from Victoria via Australia, New Zealand, Brazil, the Cape of Good Hope and the Azores to his final destination—the English seaside town of Margate.

The town's **Art Gallery** (on Wilspencer Place south of Fort Street) has works of the English Impressionist Walter Sickert, French water-colourist Eugène Boudin and Dutch landscape-painter of the 17th century, Adrian Van de Velde.

One delightful excursion outside Victoria, an easy bus-ride, will take you to what is the ultimate comment on this floral fairyland—**Butchart Gardens.** Robert Pim Butchart made a fortune out of Portland cement and found himself stuck with an exhausted limestone quarry 13 miles north of Victoria. His wife suggested turning the whole huge thing into a garden. The result is an almost bewilderingly beautiful phantasmagoria of fountains, lakes, rockeries, trees and flowers: the **Sunken Garden,** with its symmetrical Trees of Life and rockery of gentians, saxifrage and Lebanon candy tuft; the **Rose Garden,** at its best in July—150 varieties of hybrid tea and floribunda roses; the **Japanese Garden,** with its scarlet azaleas, Himalayan *blue* poppies, weeping larch tree and a pond with a couple of cranes for good luck; and the dreamy **Italian Garden,** cypress trees singing a song of Tuscany around a cruciform basin filled with water lilies where once was Mr. and Mrs. Butchart's tennis court.

Eden, Naples or Cemetery?

Victoria seems to provoke a disconcerting range of reactions in its visitors. When James Douglas came upon the spot where he was to build the new west coast base of operations for his Hudson's Bay Company, he waxed positively lyrical. In a letter of 1843 he wrote: "The place itself appears a perfect Eden, in the midst of the dreary wilderness of the North-West Coast, and so different is its general aspect, from the wooded, rugged regions around, that one might be pardoned for supposing it had dropped from the clouds into its present position."

Rudyard Kipling visited Victoria in 1907 and, with the insouciant snobbery of the incorrigible place-dropper, he wrote home: "To realize Victoria you must take all that the eye admires most in Bourne-mouth, Torquay, the Isle of Wight, the Happy Valley at Hong Kong, the Doon, Sorrento, and Camps Bay; add reminiscences of the Thousand Islands, and arrange the whole around the Bay of Naples, with some Himalayas for the background." Few manage to work that one out.

But a favourite B.C. barroom joke insists: "Victoria is God's waiting room. It is the only cemetery in the entire world with street lighting."

This view was shared by Stephen Leacock, Canadian economist and humorist (only in Canada are economists considered to be humorists), who said in a 1936 speech, from the safety of Vancouver: "In Victoria the people turn over in the morning to read the daily obituary column. Those who do not find their names there, fall back and go to sleep again."

VANCOUVER

Canada

Introduction

Vancouver is the city of Canada's 20th century, the serene achievement of its westward expansion. It personifies the good life to be had on the Pacific Ocean.

As you approach from the sea, you'll see one of those natural sites given only to a blessed few cities—an élite club with Rio de Janeiro, Sydney and San Francisco among its prominent members. This town lying in a bay embraced by soaring green mountains is sometimes reproached by detractors "back East" for being a trifle smug about itself and indifferent about the rest of the world. But if you get a taste of its gentle ambience, its clever combination of the comforts of sophisticated modernity with the simpler joys of the wilderness at its back door, you can easily imagine how it could encourage a certain self-satisfaction.

Other Canadian cities, like Toronto or Montreal, have known a more spectacular industrial or commercial growth, but Vancouver, expanding at a purposeful but more leisurely pace, has never lost sight of the importance of enjoying life at the same time.

Symbolic of this is the fact that before it took the worthy name of one of the region's first explorers—George Vancouver (see box)—the place was known as Gastown, after a saloon-keeper named "Gassy Jack" Deighton, who looked after the needs of the pioneer lumbermen in the 1860s.

If modern developers have left little of the 19th-century town, the bold contemporary designs of the Law Courts, the Simon Fraser and UBC campuses and downtown commercial buildings are a delight for architecture buffs. And there's Canada Place, the futuristic cruise terminal resembling an elegant ocean liner with sails, which juts proudly out into Burrard Inlet.

The main downtown area covers the peninsula between Burrard Inlet on the north and the Fraser River to the south. Greater Vancouver, with a population of well over a million, includes the townships of Burnaby and New Westminster and the North Shore suburbs that nestle against Grouse Mountain, Hollyburn Peak and Black Mountain, all over 4,000 feet high.

The houses of the North

George's Pitt-Fall

George Vancouver was a splendid navigator, determined explorer, but not, according to the men under his command, the nicest fellow you could wish to meet. A hard taskmaster, haughty, arrogant and mean—that was the general verdict. Still, he did meticulously chart the region that was to become the city's port area and the British were not inclined to name the place "Narvaez" or "Alcala-Galiano" after one of the Spanish seamen who'd been there before him or about the same time. George was born in 1757 in King's Lynn, England, of fine old Dutch ancestry, the Van Coeverdens. At age 28, he sailed with Captain Cook to the Pacific coast of North America and out to the Hawaiian islands, where he became a close friend of King Kamehameha. It was George who gave him the Union Jack that is still incorporated in Hawaii's state flag today. In 1791 he was sent back to the Pacific to stop the Spanish claim to exclusive rights over the territory that is now British Columbia. The voyage, which engaged in the first detailed exploration and charting of the B.C. coast, took him four years and 65,000 miles around the Pacific and Atlantic Oceans. Maritime historians agree now that in his work in mapping the Pacific coastlines, George was second only to Cook himself. The gratitude he might reasonably have expected was diluted by a problem he'd had out in Hawaii with an insubordinate midshipman. After goading George to a fury, the fellow was left ashore. Trouble was his name was Thomas Pitt, a too-close relative of John Pitt, Prime Minister. Poor George had to retire on half-pay, two months after returning from the Pacific. He died at the age of 40.

Shore represent some of the most elegant residential architecture in North America, enhanced, of course, by their superb view down the mountain side over English Bay and the Burrard Inlet.

Around the bay are splendid beaches. The sailing is first class, the fishing pure joy, and for tourists, the greenery of Stanley Park and Queen Elizabeth Gardens offers dreamy tranquillity.

Whatever cosmopolitan atmosphere the city has acquired derives from its position as a port of world importance on the Pacific Ocean, western terminus of the Canadian Pacific Railway and now the Trans-Canadian Highway.

Next stop after Vancouver is Japan and China, and the Chinese, who helped build the railway and the Japanese, who participated in the city's commercial expansion, are important parts of the urban community. Germans, Scandinavians, Italians and Ukrainians also colour the city's life, but the Anglo-Saxons remain the strongest influence.

The Pacific coast turns them more towards the United States, south to Seattle

"Pleasure first, then work" could be leisurely Vancouver's motto.

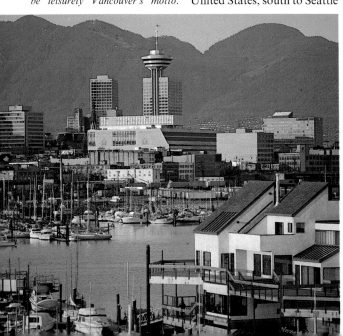

and beyond that to California, rather than across the Rocky Mountains to Alberta or further east to the French influence of Quebec. Vancouver, say its critics, is too American, not Canadian enough. Vancouver, say its residents, is whatever's your pleasure— the colour and spice of the Orient, the genteel culture of the Europeans or the more aggressive American way.

Whatever's your pleasure.

A Brief History

Pre-conquest–18th century	Before European exploration, the peninsula between Burrard Inlet and Fraser River is inhabited by Coast Salish Indians. Spanish under José Maria Narvaez discover Strait of Georgia west of the peninsula. The next year, in 1791, Captain George Vancouver explores the inlet during his coastal survey. No permanent European settlement for another 70 years.
19th century	Brief, unsuccessful attempts at coal mining leave only the name Coal Harbour (south-east of Stanley Park) as a relic in 1859. First white settlers in what is now city's West End. Sawmills sprout on both sides of Burrard Inlet. South shore's Hastings Mill becomes the nucleus of future city, then known as Gastown, after hotel- and saloon-keeper Gassy Jack Deighton.
	Two years after Coal Harbour has been chosen as western terminus for Canadian Pacific Railway, the new city of Vancouver is incorporated in April 1886. Two months later the little town is destroyed by fire inside one hour. By the end of the year, the 5,000 inhabitants have rebuilt their houses, with 50 shops, 14 office buildings, 23 hotels, nine saloons and one church, in time for the first transcontinental passenger train, May 23, 1887. International passenger liners begin docking at Vancouver in August, 1887.
20th century	Opening of the Panama Canal brings faster access to European markets and gives Vancouver's port world status.
	Greater Vancouver's population passes the one million mark in 1971.

Sightseeing

Vancouver is a very modern city, so you mustn't expect to find venerable old monuments. The fire of 1886 got rid of all but one of the pioneer buildings and modern developers have done away with most of the edifices that graced the town at the turn of the century. But the contemporary architecture is attractive enough to make a tour of the city well worth while. In addition, the museums in the downtown area and out at the University of British Columbia give a fine guide to the city's and region's past.

For a total view, take the aerial tramway operating on **Grouse Mountain.** The city's magnificent parks and beaches offer the perfect place to relax at the end of the tour.

Best place to start downtown is at **Robson Square,** where the **Law Courts** designed by master architect Arthur Erickson have given the city centre a sparkling new focus. The building, linked to the old Court House, spreads out in tiers of glassed-in walkways, offices and courtrooms and open plazas festooned with trees and shrubs, a place cool in summer and offering a rare touch of colour in the winter. Stairways run across the plazas from corner to corner in an intriguing pattern of constant visual movement.

The structure houses, down in its basement, the Vancouver tourist information centre, **Tourism British Columbia,** useful for a first orientation around the city.

Robson Square also provides a new home for the **Vancouver Art Gallery.** The star feature of this collection of Canadian artists is the splendid work of Emily Carr. "Crazy Old Millie" as she was locally known—"Klee Wyck" or the "Laughing One" to the Indians—was frequently to be seen wheeling her pet monkey in a pram around the streets of Victoria. But her bizarre behaviour in no way detracted from the quality of her boldly coloured landscapes. Clearly influenced by the French Post-Impressionists with whom she studied, they are unmistakably British Columbian in subject-matter, frequently depicting totem poles in their natural settings.

On the north-west corner of the square, at Granville and Georgia, is **Birks Clock,** a strange enough contraption to look at but more important

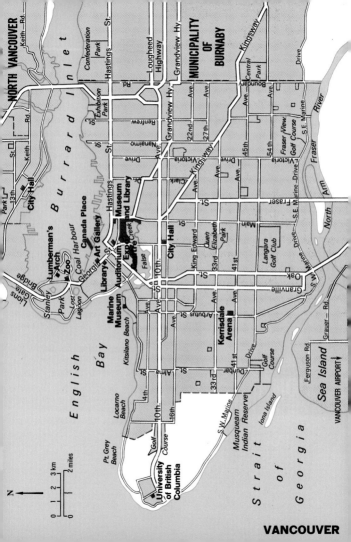

NORTH VANCOUVER

MUNICIPALITY OF BURNABY

Keith Rd.

13th St.

Confederation Park

Hastings St.

Lougheed Highway

Grandview Hy.

Kingsway

Burrard Inlet

Exhibition Park

Renfrew St.

Boundary Rd.

Central Park

Fraser River

Keith Rd.

City Hall

Nanaimo St.

22nd Ave.

27th Ave.

S.E. Marine Drive

45th Ave.

Fraser View Golf Course

54th Ave.

Drive

Victoria Drive

Kingsway

Park La.

Lions Gate Bridge

Stanley Park

Lost Lagoon

Lumberman's Arch

Zoo

Coal Harbour

Canada Place

Georgia Art Gallery

Hastings

Museum and Library

Clark Drive

Victoria Drive

Fraser St.

S.E. Marine Drive

North Arm

Library

Marine Museum

Auditorium

Expo Creek Site

False Creek

City Hall

Main St.

King Edward Ave.

Queen Elizabeth Park

33rd Ave.

41st Ave.

Langara Golf Club

Kitsilano Beach

Arbutus St.

10th Ave.

Kerrisdale Arena

Oak St.

Granville St.

S.W. Marine Drive

Grauer Rd.

Alma St.

Dunbar St.

41st Ave.

33rd Ave.

Golf Course

Drive

Ferguson Rd.

English Bay

Locarno Beach

4th Ave.

10th Ave.

16th Ave.

S.W. Marine Drive

Sea Island

VANCOUVER AIRPORT

Pt. Grey Beach

Golf Course

Musqueam Indian Reserve

Iona Island

University of British Columbia

N

0 1 2 3 km
0   1   2 miles

Strait of Georgia

VANCOUVER

as a favourite landmark for downtown rendezvous.

Further east, in the area around Pender Street is Vancouver's cosmopolitan pride and joy, **Chinatown.** Second in size in North America only to San Francisco's, the Chinese community here is cheerful at play in the *mah-jong* parlours and earnest at work in the fruit and vegetable markets, fishmongers', spice merchants' and the shops of traditional silks, satins and bamboo wares from Hong Kong, Taiwan and mainland China.

The windows of the myriad restaurants display their glistening lacquered barbecued pork and poultry. The street décor is everywhere colourful, even the telephone booths have pagoda-style roofs. The new **Chinese Cultural Centre** includes a park and garden at the corner of Pender and Carrall, with pavilions, bridges, hillocks and terraces landscaped by specialists brought in from Suchou, west of Shanghai.

Towards the harbour and railyards, is the resuscitated

Saloon-owner "Gassy Jack" Deighton lent his name to fun district.

district of Vancouver's beginnings, **Gastown** (between Water and Hastings). This merchant's paradise of bustling boutiques, souvenir shops, bars and restaurants is frankly commercial in its polished quaintness but nonetheless attractive in its cheerful atmosphere.

(The only remnant from the original Gastown to have survived the 1886 fire is the **Old Hastings Mill Store** at 1575 Alma Road near Jericho Beach, nicely restored as a museum for turn-of-the-century paraphernalia.)

Characteristic of the town's taste for the good things of life is the way it has just recently turned seedy industrial facilities festering on the waterfront into the delightfully innovative residential district of **False Creek.** Overlooking it is the spectacular 170-acre setting of Expo 86—70 pavilions and plazas crowned by a phenomenal 17-storey geodesic sphere, the Expo Centre itself.

A knack for incorporating natural beauty in an urban setting is epitomized in **Stanley Park.** Created in 1889 and named after the then Governor-General of Canada, Lord Stanley, this park, with its majestic old 300-foot Douglas firs, cedars and Sitka spruce,

92

Fur Better or Fur Worse

There's an all too convenient image of the Indians first encountered by Captain Cook off the coast of Vancouver Island. Paddling out with offerings of sea-otter skins and other furs in exchange for whatever beads or bits of metal the British sailors cared to toss them, the Indians provided a facile example of naive natives exploited by venal white men.

Recent studies of the fur trade's early days show that this picture does a disservice to the Indians and overestimates the wiles of the Europeans. The Kwakiutl Indians of British Columbia in fact proved very skilful traders, quickly gauging what they could really get for their furs in iron, copper and brass, in chisels and axes, and constantly raising the price according to very real market conditions of supply and demand.

One British trader, John Meares, noted ruefully in 1790: "We found to our cost that these people possessed all the cunning necessary to the gains of mercantile life." Besides which, their own beads were vastly superior to what the, Europeans had to offer.

Whether approached by sea or air, Vancouver's site is breathtaking.

its delightful rose-garden, zoo, aquarium, bowling greens, cricket field (this is *British* Columbia) and open-air theatre makes an enchanting sanctuary to flee to from city noise.

At Brockton Point, on the eastern end of the park, you can meditate beneath the clus-

ter of totem poles. From Prospect Point, at the north tip of the promontory jutting out into Vancouver Harbour, you can sit and watch the oil-tankers and grain cargo ships bound for Japan, China and the Soviet Union, much more than a world away. Or fall asleep on one of the beaches on the western side of the park facing the afternoon sun.

Vancouver is very much a garden city, as you will see if you drive past the immaculately kept lawns of the residential districts. For public enjoyment there are the **Queen Elizabeth Gardens** (at Cambie and East 33rd Avenue) with

Poles Apart

The myths shrouding totem poles derive almost more from the popular imagination of white man than from the Indians themselves. For instance, not all Indian tribes make totem poles. In its authentic form, it is an art peculiar to the West Coast of North America, centred principally on northern British Columbia around the Nass and Skeena Rivers and on the Pacific islands.

Totem poles are not an ancient art form. The huge free-standing carved red cedar poles erected in front of Indian homes are essentially a 19th-century phenomenon, dependent for their multiplicity of intricate carving on the chisels, steel axes, curved knives and other metal tools introduced to the Indians by European traders. Size was previously limited to that of the poles and beams needed for the structure of the house itself to which the carvings were directly attached. When their trade in sea-otter skins declined in mid-19th century, the Indians could no longer rely on the opulence of their personal possessions with which to proclaim their prestige, so they resorted to bigger and better totem poles. On the Nass River, poles began to soar to 80 feet and more. In the 1880s, Chief Hladerh of the Wolves had Chief Sispegoot of the Killer-Whales murdered for daring to erect a totem pole taller than his.

Lastly, totem poles are not monuments of deities or devils to be worshipped (as Christian missionaries believed when they ordered them destroyed). They are illustrations of ancestral symbols—Eagle, Frog, Raven, Bear, Whale and Wolf being the most common—and commemorate historical events. A totem pole is in the truest sense a family-tree complete with the heroic deeds of uncles, aunts and grandpas. Some tribes even interred the ashes of their family inside the poles.

the tropical plants of its Bloedel Conservatory, and the **Van Dusen Botanical Gardens** (Oak Street). These have a very fine collection of miniature Japanese bonzai trees.

The small Vanier Park (north of Burrard Street) has two museums. The **Centennial Museum** contains an interesting collection of regional history and ethnology. Particularly charming are the Chilkat blankets of interwoven goat's wool and cedar bark. In the **Maritime Museum,** pride of place is given to the *Saint-Roch*, the

Modern architecture at its most effective at a modern shopping-centre.

noble vessel of the Royal Canadian Mounted Police which from 1940 to 1944 made a historic voyage clear around the North American continent via the Panama Canal and the Arctic Ocean, hunting German U-Boats on the way.

But perhaps the most impressive museum in Vancouver is the University of British Columbia's **Museum of Anthropology,** out at the western end of the Vancouver peninsula on Point Grey overlooking the Strait of Georgia. First of all, it's a good excuse for visiting one of the most beautiful college campuses in North America. The terraced Sedgwick Library and the Faculty Club rose garden are two gems in a superb setting of sea and mountain backdrop. The museum itself is another masterpiece by Erickson, a structure whose 20th-century glass and concrete are cannily reminiscent of the great old Indian post-and-beam long houses. Outside, as of old, the reconstructed Haida Indian houses and more recently carved but nonetheless authentic totem poles face the great Pacific Ocean rather than huddling in the unnatural confinement of musty museum walls.

The glassed-in Great Hall of the museum is itself a miracle of light providing a free and airy shelter for the older 40-foot Tsimshian and Kwakiutl poles and house-front figures. Look out for the huge wooden feast-dishes, big as bathtubs, used to dispense food at the great "potlatch" ceremonies at which the tribes proclaimed their greatness by the munificence of their hospitality.

The museum is frequently host to traditional Indian salmon-bakes and festivities surrounding the erection of a new totem pole. With the recent revival of Indian culture, this is by no means an artificial tourist-inspired gimmick, since totemism is part of the B.C. Indians' very recent past and present.

To complete your picture of Vancouver's idyllic setting, you should drive across **Lions' Gate Bridge** from Stanley Park to the elegant suburbs of North and West Vancouver. Wind your way in among the dazzling mountainside mansions of **British Properties** at the end of Taylor Way. The view over the bay and the Vancouver peninsula is, as every guide-book is allowed to say at least once, breathtaking. If you have time, take the magnificent coastal road along Marine Drive past more superb houses, gardens and parkland, towards Horseshoe Bay. You'll understand why Vancouverites don't give too much thought to the rest of the world.

"Timber-r-r-r!"

Today's lumberjack ain't what he used to be. In the "good" old days, he hiked his way out to British Columbia's endless wilderness to hole up for six months at a time in isolated lumber camps in a gloomy windowless log cabin, emerging only to chop down everything in sight, stripping whole forests bare. He shaved with his axe as a razor, ate salt pork and beans for lunch and beans and salt pork for dinner. Women were barred from the camp because, it was said, he might get distracted and chop off a finger.

Now he commutes to the forest in a station-wagon, fells his quota of trees with a power-saw as directed by forestry-scientists who have carefully selected the trees by computer-programmed surveys, and then drives home each night to his house in the suburbs. You can't shave with a power-saw.

A Salmon Primer

The salmon, insist the sportsmen, is the noblest fish of them all. And the Pacific salmon is the monarch. In fact, what the Canadians call "chinook", the largest and feistiest of these fish, is known to the Americans quite simply as King Salmon.

There are five species of Pacific salmon—sockeye, pink, coho, chum (or "dog") and chinook (or king). They begin life in freshwater, grow and mature in the ocean and return to freshwater to spawn and then to die.

The *sockeye* is the best known of the food fish. It's bright red, rich in oil and holds its colour and flavour for processing.

It spawns in tributary streams above a lake and the hatched young or small fry makes its way down to the lake to grow on a diet of water fleas to a length of 3 to 4 inches. After one or two years, it's ready for the ocean, making a journey of as much as 1,000 miles. After three summers at sea, feeding off shrimp, it returns weighing 5 to 7 pounds to its native river to spawn. This last migration takes it unerringly to the original stream where it began as an egg four years earlier. At the spawning ground it scours a nest or redd, deposits its eggs and dies, almost immediately. In the gravel bed of the stream, the new cycle begins the following spring, when the young hatch and make their way down to the lake...

The *coho* is a champion high jumper. It could clear a bar 11 feet high (compared with man's world record of just over 7 feet). It has dark red flesh and a deep red, even sometimes blue back. Reaching 3 feet or more in length, it can weigh from 10 to 25 pounds.

This and the *chinook* are the best of the sports fish, most willing to take the troller's lure in salt water at the mouth of their river during the spawning months of July, August and September. The chinook reaches a weight of 20 to 25 pounds after 4 years at sea, 40 pounds after 5 years.

In this league, the *pink* is a minnow. The *chum* is also known as *dog* because Indians, seafood gourmets in this region, feed it only to their dogs. In fact, it's perfectly palatable when smoked.

PRINCE RUPERT
WITH THE INLAND PASSAGE

Canada

Introduction

Prince Rupert is a living example of British Columbia's pioneering days. It's a perfect natural harbour, ice-free all year round, providing an ideal distribution point for the province's fisheries, mining and logging industries.

The port's position on Kaien Island at the mouth of the Skeena River and across the Hecate Strait from the Queen Charlotte Islands has also made it a natural focus for the finest of British Columbia's Indian art. The exquisite black argillite carvings of the Haida Indians have come from the islands while totem pole art reached its apogee among the Tsimshian Indians of the Skeena River.

And Prince Rupert's special bonus is that the sea approach from the south takes you through the beautiful Inland Passage, close by the tree-lined eastern coast-line of Vancouver Island and the nordic fjords of the British Columbian mainland. The journey gives you a keen visual sense of just what an "outpost of civilisation" can mean.

A Brief History

1906	Scouting party for the Grand Trunk Pacific Railway chooses Kaien Island as site for its western terminus (now northern branch line of Canadian National Railway—CNR).
1907	Railway workers' camp is set up as precursor to Prince Rupert.
1912	Grand Trunk Pacific reaches Prince Rupert in the same year that the *Titanic* sinks with Prince Rupert's founder Charles Hays aboard, along with his port-expansion plans.
1942–45	Town's full importance is realised when Prince Rupert's port facilities are used by United States Army in World War II.
1945–83	Expansion of canning, lumber and area mining facilities. New coal port constructed.

Sightseeing

Inland Passage

The 280-mile-long **Vancouver Island** is the largest of British Columbia's Pacific islands and is covered with snow-capped mountains and dense pine-forest, source of much of the province's wealth.

North of Victoria and due west of the city of Vancouver is **Nanaimo,** an increasingly important port-city but still best known for something weird that happens there every year in mid-July: the World Championship Bathtub Race from Nanaimo 17 miles across the Strait of Georgia to Vancouver. Rest assured, the tubs are powered with outboard motors, but they're genuine bathtubs escorted by properly seaworthy motorboats in case someone inadvertently pulls the plug. Anthropologists are also intrigued by the petroglyphs found around Nanaimo, carvings in the local sandstone similar to those found on the Hawaiian Islands over 2,600 miles away.

Equally reminiscent of Hawaii are the lovely white sands of **Qualicum Beach,** a favourite islanders' resort.

Campbell River is the site of an annual Salmon Festival, also in July. These were originally the Indian fishermen's equivalent of the farmers' harvest festivals, to ensure a good catch and safe fishing. There are still propitiatory dances, traditional and modern, a salmon derby and war-canoe races. The catch is usually better for it all.

At the head of the Strait of Georgia is **Quadra Island,** named after the Spanish navigator Bodega y Quadro, whom George Vancouver persuaded to relinquish Spain's exclusive claim to the Pacific coastal territory in 1792.

Goodbye, Charlie

The man who saw the possibilities of the place was Charles Hays, general manager of the Grand Trunk Pacific Railway. He named the town after enterprising Prince Rupert, cousin of King Charles II of England and founding governor of the Hudson's Bay Company. The town was made the railway's western terminus and Hays went off to Europe to look for investors. Unfortunately, he came back on the *Titanic*. The great promise of Prince Rupert's looming prosperity collided with that iceberg and went down with Charlie Hays. Prince Rupert took a whole generation to recover.

Along the B.C. mainland, you'll pass the spectacularly rugged coastline, with the fjord of the **Toba** and **Bute** Inlets. The Bute Inlet is the mouth of the Homathko River leading back 50 miles inland to British Columbia's highest mountain, the 13,260-foot Mount Waddington.

Back on Vancouver Island, **Kelsey Bay** offers wild forest scenery around this major centre of the logging industry. The community clusters at the point where the White and Salmon Rivers join and flow together into the Johnstone Strait.

On Cormorant Island, **Alert Bay,** like Victoria, boasts the world's tallest totem-pole. The salmon they catch here are big, too.

Port Hardy, northernmost commercial harbour on Vancouver Island, celebrates in August its FI-LO-MI Days, in honour of the three local industries—fishing, logging and mining.

Prince Rupert

The **harbour** itself is a fascinating show to start with. You're likely to come across a very cosmopolitan mixture of sailors—Greeks, Italians, Russians, Chinese, Sikh Indians, even a few British. After wandering among the trawlers, grain-cargoes, yachts and pleasure-launches, you can make your way up to Roosevelt Park for a fine overview of the whole harbour from the grain elevator across to the Yacht Club—and beyond to the Tsimshian Peninsula and Chatham Sound.

Franklin D. Roosevelt Park was dedicated to the United States President in honour of the U.S. Army's war effort after Prince Rupert's port fa-

cilities had played an important role as a staging area for the Pacific theatre of operations. (The harbour was in part mined and covered with netting to prevent a sea-version of the Pearl Harbor attack.) Over 50,000 American troops passed through Prince Rupert during the war— 7,000 at a time stationed here. Known by locals as "Little America", the army's HQ was housed where the park has now been laid out.

The **Museum of Northern British Columbia** (which also contains the Visitors' Information Bureau) traces 10,000 years of regional history, since the first settlers came down the Pacific coast after crossing over the Bering Strait from Asia. There are excellent pieces of Indian, Aleut and Eskimo artwork, together with a few comparable pieces from Australia, New Zealand, Asia and Africa.

Artistically, perhaps the

most beautiful work is in the gleaming black argillite carvings of totemic animals by Haida Indians from the Queen Charlotte Islands. One fascinating item is an Indian "bent box", a sort of pantry or larder that has been bent into shape from a single piece of wood by a process of steaming and cutting to fit the box together. You can also see the tools and weapons used in the 19th-century sea otter skin-trade at nearby Fort Simpson.

In front of the museum and throughout the town stand many interesting examples of Haida and Tsimshian totem poles—remember that this area is the probable birthplace of the art of the totem pole. Behind the museum is a **carving shed** in which, as in Victoria's Thunderbird Park, Indians still work on their ancient sculptural skills.

Next time you come across a Sunken Garden, find out what it was *before*. In Victoria, the one in the gorgeous Butchart Gardens grew out of a disused limestone quarry. In Prince Rupert, the **Sunken Garden** at the back of the Provincial Courthouse grew out of a mistake. The city fathers had the foundations for the courthouse dug in the wrong place. They moved the site to its present location and turned the ugly gaping hole into this really very pretty garden of shrubs and flowers and fanciful rockeries. Quite a few convicted local burglars would like to see the same thing happen to the present courthouse site.

Courthouses have never been popular in Prince Rupert, as attested by the delicious tale behind the bright but unprepossessing Besner Block (corner of 3rd Street and 3rd Avenue, nice totem pole in front). The Besner was built in 1928 by an exceedingly popular businessman named Olier Besner. Ollie was popular because he had a very tasty sideline in bootlegging alcohol. He was convicted and sent off to jail in Vancouver and the townspeople escorted him to the dockside with an honourable torchlit procession. Vancouver understood these things better, quashed the conviction, and Ollie returned to Prince Rupert in triumph.

Two of the town's major industries offer tours of their factories. You can visit the **cannery** and watch fresh sal-

Watch the day's catch go directly from the sea and into a can—fast.

mon come in from the boats and end up, in a process you follow on a 20-minute tour, in a tin-can with a neat pink label. If that is too painful a thought, try the **pulp mill,** where you watch the lumber turned into wood-pulp.

If that's too painful, too, get away from it all on the **Mount Hays** Sky Ride. You'll see that lumber in its beautiful natural state in the forests surrounding the 1,864-foot mountain. Bears and deer occasionally emerge from the forest but you stand a much better chance of seeing eagles flying around the mountain's summit. You get to the top in a gondola cablecar. To the west, you'll see the Queen Charlotte Islands across the Hecate Strait and to the north, the mountainous beginnings of the Alaska Panhandle.

KETCHIKAN

Alaska, U.S.A.

Introduction

You won't understand Ketchikan if you don't make an imaginative leap out of the mundane realities of life. At first sight of the pleasant sleepy little town sprawling along the waterfront on the west coast of Revillagegido Island, you may wonder how it earned its dramatic name of "Thundering Wings of an Eagle", which is what Ketchikan means in Tlingit Indian. But if you climb up 3,000-foot Deer Mountain overlooking the town, you'll see how Ketchikan spreads along the seashore in the shape of the original Tlingit summer fishing camp—the distinctive form of an eagle in full flight.

And how come little Ketchikan also calls itself Alaska's First City when in fact it is by no means the oldest and is much smaller than Juneau, Fairbanks or Anchorage? Well, everybody likes to be first in something, and Ketchikan just happens to be the first town the ships come to along the Inland Passage from the south.

Granted, but what about this boast, lit up in a permanent banner across the city's main street: "Salmon Capital of the World"? Admittedly, the local fishing industry declined sharply after World War II and was supplanted in the 1950s by timber and pulp mills. But in the 1930s there were 11 canneries in operation, turning out nearly 2 million cases of salmon a year and in those days nobody could beat that. In the fish business, Ketchikan may not be the biggest any more, but the locals insist that their king salmon still tastes the best.

The American residents seem to have wholeheartedly adopted the fanciful turn of mind of Ketchikan's original settlers, the Tlingit Indians. Perhaps the most important totemic symbol of the Tlingits is the raven, regarded as the legendary ancestor of the whole tribe. So a young Tlingit boy was understandably disturbed to hear in his Ketchikan school's biology class that he was not descended from the Great Nass River Raven, as his father had told him. But his father insisted: "*You* were descended from the raven. The white man may be descended from the monkey, but *you* were descended from the raven".

And Ketchikan, "Thundering Wings of an Eagle", is Alaska's First City, Salmon Capital of the World.

A Brief History

19th century	Ketchikan or "Kitschk-him" begins as a Tlingit summer fishing camp until white Americans arrive to exploit the salmon fisheries for the Tongass Packing Company in 1887. Like other south-eastern Alaska towns, Ketchikan grows as a result of the gold boom, with substantial finds in nearby hills and on Prince of Wales Island.
20th century	Ketchikan is incorporated as a mining town in 1900. A customs house is set up to make Ketchikan Alaska's first port of entry. Gold and copper mines close down during World War I and salmon fishing takes over as the town's major industry. Ketchikan serves as an important U.S. Coast Guard base in World War II. The fisheries decline in the 1940s and the Ketchikan Pulp Company and Spruce Mill make timber the new chief source of revenue.

Sightseeing

Whatever the cynics may say, the fisheries are still very active in Ketchikan and the **docks** are a delightful place to hang around and watch the boats bringing in their catch — herring and halibut as well as salmon.

When you stroll around town, you mustn't miss colourful **Creek Street,** with its boardwalk running alongside the old houses built up on pilings above Ketchikan Creek. As has been said before, Ketchikanners are proud of the strangest things, and Creek Street is much revered hereabouts as the great red-light district of the town's mining days when a house was just a home for Frenchie, Dolly, Black Mary and Blind Polly. A sign tells you this was once "the most infamous red light district in Alaska" — it would scarcely do to be less than the most infamous — adding: "the only place in the world where both the fish and the fishermen went up the stream to spawn". From time to time, **Dolly's House,** complete with scarlet satin-covered four-poster brass bed and elegant tapestried walls, is still thrown open to the public — sightseeing only.

For a theatrical version of the goings-on in Creek Street and other Ketchikan harbour hanky-panky, you can see a performance at the downtown **Frontier Saloon** of the melodrama "The Fish Pirate's Daughter".

Surprisingly, Creek Street also manages to concern itself with more serious cultural pursuits. The Tongass Historical Society Museum houses more than 1,000 exhibits of the Tlingit, Tsimshian and Haida Indian cultures, together with pioneer memorabilia and wildlife displays.

Other serious art forms can be enjoyed at the **Totem Heritage Cultural Centre** on Deermount Avenue. The centre has salvaged and preserved marvellously weather-beaten totem poles from surrounding Tlingit and Haida villages.

You'll notice the pride of place given to the raven in the hierarchy of totemic symbols. Tlingit Indian legends tell how the Great Raven inhabited the upper firmament, watching over the lights of the cosmos, the sun, the moon and the stars. His grandson, the Scamp Raven, famous for his beneficent rascalry, stole first the stars, then the moon and finally the sun and handed them over to mankind.

The totemic tradition is continued with fine replicas of Tlingit poles, along with an Indian community-house, in a tranquil open-air setting out at **Totem Bight Park,** 10 miles to the north, and at **Saxman Totem Park,** a couple of miles south of Ketchikan. Look carefully at the totemic faces and you'll see how the human features blend into the eyes and beaks of a bird or a bear, subtly illustrating the symbiotic relationship between the Indians and their animal counterparts.

It's always a nicely perverse pleasure to watch other people hard at work while you're on holiday. On your way back from Totem Bight Park, the North Tongass Highway takes you past **Ward Cove,** home of the Ketchikan Pulp Company. There in the narrows, trees felled at 26 nearby logging camps are formed into vast log-rafts.

SITKA

Alaska, U.S.A.

Introduction

Sitka is Alaska's little piece of Russia. This is a historical rather than a visual fact, though there is the onion dome of the reconstructed Russian Orthodox St. Michael's Cathedral, and brightly costumed "New Archangel" traditional Russian dancers come down to meet the cruise ships on the dockside. Otherwise there are few recognizable remains of the town of New Archangel that the Russian-American Company's general-manager Alexander Baranov founded in 1799 to exploit the fur trade in sea otter skins. The Tlingit Indians, whose village had been razed to make way for it, referred to the site merely as "this place"—Sitka.

Despite the ravages of time and the ups and downs of a difficult economic development, the place derives considerable charm both from local pride in its historical significance as Alaska's first capital and from its picturesque setting on the west coast of Baranov Island facing the romantic silhouette of Mount Edgecumbe on Kruzof Island.

A tour of Sitka will give you a concentrated sense of three important facets of the Alaskan adventure: from the docks where the Russians loaded their furs to be sent off to China, up to the parade ground on Castle Hill where they handed the territory over to the United States in 1867, and around the National Historical Park with its totemic carvings of the Tlingit Indians who were here long before these strange, tough, enterprising white men—and may still outlast them.

Some Local Disturbances

To say the least, Alaska is a land of dramatic extremes in its natural phenomena. One June day in 1912, Mount Katmai, covered with snow and glaciers like any other self-respecting Alaskan mountain, was decapitated by a volcanic eruption which hurled 5½ cubic miles of debris into the air. The town of Kodiak, 100 miles away, was inundated with volcanic ash and plunged into total darkness for 60 hours—this in the land of the midnight sun. The explosion was heard in Juneau, 750 miles away, and sulphuric acid particles disintegrated cloth fabric down in Seattle, 2000 miles away. As part of the Pacific Rim earthquake zone, since 1788 Alaska has known 880 earthquakes that would measure more than 5 points on the Richter scale (maximum 9).

A Brief History

1799	With the decline of sea otter supplies in the Aleutians, Alexander Baranov explores Panhandle for new base of operations. The Russian-American Company, modelled on British East India Company, a private firm with limited governmental powers, is established near present-day Sitka with Baranov as its first general manager. It is named Michailovsk.
19th century	Tlingit Indians massacre Russian colony in 1802 while Baranov is away at Kodiak Island. He returns two years later with reinforcements and the Russian warship *Neva* assists in the destruction of the Tlingit village. On that site, Sitka, Baranov builds New Archangel, capital of Russian America.
	Baranov is replaced in 1817 as de facto governor of Alaska. He dies in Batavia on his way back to Russia. The Russian navy takes command at Sitka.
	In 1830 under Baron Ferdinand Wrangell (an Estonian German), life in Sitka makes an attempt at St. Petersburg-style gaiety, with balls and banquets organized by Baroness Elizabeth.
	U.S. Secretary of State William H. Seward negotiates purchase of Alaska in 1867 for $ 7,200,000, a deal dismissed by American press as "Seward's Folly", "Seward's Iceberg" and "Walrussia". October 18—now celebrated as Alaska Day—the Imperial Russian flag is lowered at Sitka and replaced by the Stars and Stripes. Russians are offered American citizenship. Most go home, some stay and others go to California. German-born entrepreneur George Pilz sends a couple of prospectors down to the Gastineau Channel to look for gold in 1880. They find some and the result is that the town of Juneau, mushrooming up on the spot, inexorably takes over from Sitka as capital of Alaska.
20th century	The capital's administration is formally moved out of Sitka in 1906.
	After years of desultory attempts to make salmon-fisheries lucrative, pulp mills are built around Sitka to put logging on a firm footing as a basis for the town's economy. Along with tourism.

Czar of Alaska

If he'd been an American, Alexander Baranov might have become a great folk hero. But the Russians, not being particularly proud of letting Alaska slip through their fingers, have let the fellow, who was virtual king of this vast territory for nearly 20 years, sink into oblivion. He was a lusty, hard-drinking, life-loving man, with just the right amount of melancholy in his soul to make him good meat for a Dostoievsky. Yet he was, as he always insisted, a mere businessman, not an empire-builder; short, plump and bald—imagine Mr. Pickwick in *The Brothers Karamazov*.

His first task on arriving in Sitka in 1799 was to keep his motley crew of fur-hunters, *promyshlenniki,* happy during the long boring winters. He personally brewed them a potent concoction of crab apples, rye meal and cranberries and then himself drank them all under the table at the countless parties he threw for their birthdays, saints' days, ships' arrivals, any pretext at all. He allowed no prostitution but encouraged the men to set up house with native Aleut or Tlingit Indian women. Having left his wife and daughter behind in Russia, Baranov took as his own companion the daughter of a Kenai Indian chief—at the latter's insistence.

But it was a hard life. The Tlingits massacred the first Russian colony at Sitka while Baranov was away. A band of disgruntled *promyshlenniki* tried to assassinate him in 1809. Back in Russia, his bosses, far from appreciating his considerable efforts at expanding the fur trade, finally fired him on trumped-up embezzlement charges.

It was a sad end for a man who gave such splendid parties at that mansion they called "Baranov's Castle". He'd even organized an orchestra and composed a song that had to be performed at least once on every festive occasion. It began: "The will of our hunters, the spirit of trade/On these far shores a new Muscovy made"—and didn't get any better.

Sightseeing

Start at **St. Michael's Cathedral.** The church is moving testimony to the ability of the Russian Orthodox religion to endure where commerce and force of arms left little trace. (It is remarkable, for instance, that the Aleuts, who were ruthlessly exploited and massacred by the first Russian fur-

traders, have in their vast majority adopted the Russian Orthodox faith.)

The original cathedral was built in 1848 by Bishop Ioann Veniaminov, a great scholar and missionary among the Aleuts for whose language he developed an alphabet and grammar. The simple grey clapboard edifice with its onion dome was burned down in 1966, but the original blueprints were preserved and it was possible to reconstruct the church in exactly the same form (adding new fireproofing). The townspeople were able to rescue nearly all the priceless icons, paintings and relics now again on display. You can see a lovely 18th-century gold and bejewelled chalice, Bishop Veniaminov's mitre, a 19th-century silver-bound Bible, and altar cloths embroidered by Mariia Maksutova, wife of the last Russian governor of Alaska.

The **Bishop's House,** built a few years before St. Michael's on Crescent Harbour has now been restored. The only other Russian building, also in restored form, is the conical wooden **Blockhouse,** just off Seward Street, which served to guard the boundary between Russian and Tlingit Indian sections of town.

Up on **Castle Hill** is the original placement of the Tlingit village before it was razed by the Russians. Baranov's Castle has disappeared, but you can see the **Russian cannon** bearing the Imperial Russian two-headed eagle crest. There's a wonderful view of Sitka Sound and the flat-peaked 3,201-foot **Mount Edgecumbe.** The parade-ground where the cannon still stands was the scene of the ceremonial handing over of Alaska by the Russians to the Americans in 1867. Eyewitnesses tell how reluctant the Russian flag was to be lowered, getting stuck in the flag-staff-ropes and causing the Russian governor's wife, poor Mariia Maksutova, to swoon in an anguished faint. The U.S. flag went up with indecent unhampered haste. Each Alaska Day, October 18, the scene is re-enacted, without hitches or fainting.

On Lincoln Street, the **Sheldon Jackson Museum,** named after its Presbyterian founder, was Alaska's first concrete building (1895) and houses one of the state's finest collec-

The moose calf, a well-loved if not always friendly Alaskan.

tions of Eskimo weapons, tools and craftwork.

The **National Historical Park,** half a mile along Metlekatla Street, takes you through graceful avenues of spruce—Sitka spruce as it's properly known—and hemlock trees to a grove where you can admire a collection of 18 Tlingit and Haida **totem poles.** The tallest is the Chief Sonnihat Pole (59 feet). The site is perfect for a moment of quiet meditation, all the more poignant with the knowledge that these poles mark the spot where the Tlingits staged their last stand against the white man in Alaska, in 1804. This was where Baranov's men took their revenge for the massacre of the Mikhailovsk colony two years earlier.

Down on the waterfront in Totem Square in front of the **Centennial Building,** is a brightly painted 50-foot Tlingit war-canoe dug out of a red cedar log. Not quite a match for the Russian warship *Neva,* but more attractive. The Centennial, a convention hall and auditorium (where the traditional Russian dances are performed), also houses a nicely done scale model of 19th-century Sitka, showing the stockade wall, tanneries and other factories and the

Alaska's Silent Majority
When considering the inhabitants of this vast, still untamed land of Alaska, it's more important than in most places to remember the wildlife—they are, after all, in the majority: the *sea otter* whose beautiful skins first attracted European and American traders; the *walrus* prized for the ivory of its tusks; the *whales,* blue, grey, humpback and the all-white beluga; the *bear,* not just the polar of Arctic Alaska, but the not-so-jolly black bear and above all, the fearsome grizzly, as much a monarch in his territory as the lion in Africa or the tiger in Asia; the *salmon,* king, chum and sockeye, and *trout,* rainbow, dolly varden and steelhead; and America's national bird, in abundance on Admiralty Island, the *bald-headed eagle.*

docks and shipyards. There is a display of furniture from Baranov's Castle (a name given to all three mansions that occupied the site).

In front of **Pioneer Home,** built for pensioned-off goldprospectors—yes, still a couple left—look for the 13½-foot bronze and clay statue of William "Skagway Bill" Fonda (no relation to Henry or Jane), one of the greats of the Klondike rush.

How about 33,000 Blankets?

Before the Russians arrived in Sitka, the Tlingit Indians had lived a life of such carefree abundance that they, like other Indians of the Northwest, resorted to the ingenious ritual of "potlatch" to deal with the surplus.

Deriving from the Nootka Indian word *patschatl* meaning "to give", the potlatch enabled an Indian chief to demonstrate his prestige to his followers and more importantly to neighbouring tribes. Over a period of a year or more, he would gather up the surplus wealth of his tribe in order to throw a huge party for a neighbouring chief, to whom he would present his impressive gifts. They would eat a splendid feast and then the guest would depart knowing that in a year or two he would have to reciprocate if he was not to lose face.

His party would have to be at least as bountiful, perhaps a little more so, but not too much because that would be taken as an affront and even an act of hostility. To our way of market-economy thinking, this may not seem a very good idea for dealing with one's surplus goods. But for the Indians unworried by profits, with plenty of supplies to meet their demands, it was a means of "buying" good fellowship, peaceful relations with their neighbours and, last but by no means least, a very good party.

Originally the gifts usually consisted of oil, carvings, jewellery, blankets, whatever iron tools had been picked up from passing white men, and even slaves.

But the potlatch system died of glut when the Russians and Americans seeking sea otter furs flooded the Indians with more wealth than they could handle. Then venereal and other diseases that accompanied this excessive wealth decimated the population, and finally the bottom fell out of the fur market.

Nonetheless, vestiges of potlatch reappear from time to time when Indian community leaders throw parties at which sewing machines, refrigerators, television sets and bedspreads (more prized now than blankets) exchange hands in more numbers than can be used for anything but prestige.

JUNEAU

Alaska, U.S.A.

Introduction

Gold is what got Juneau started and Juneau is where Alaska's American story really begins. The United States took possession of Alaska in its Russian capital, Sitka, in 1867, but the territory didn't really capture the imagination of Americans until, 13 years later, a couple of drunken adventurers made their lackadaisical discovery of gold in a creek tumbling into the Gastineau Channel.

Of the town itself, what you may first notice are the taller buildings dominating the downtown area. These state and federal office buildings constitute the hub of Alaska's government—the second fact of Juneau's identity. They are the final flowering of Juneau's legislative role begun when the goldminers held their first political convention in 1881. Twenty-odd years later, Juneau became the official capital of Alaska. The proud new government buildings were defiantly erected to resist the move to transfer the state capital to Willow, a town closer to the major population centres of Anchorage and Fairbanks.

Beyond the mountains against which the town nestles, the 3,576-foot Mount Juneau and the 3,819-foot Mount Roberts, you can see the third distinctive feature of Juneau's life: the first white peaks of the Juneau Icefield, source of the glaciers that surround the city, the Mendenhall, Taku, Eagle and Herbert glaciers. The mountains provide a natural shelter against this formidable frozen barrier. They give Juneau a milder climate free of the permafrost that covers the rest of Alaska north of this southern coastal area.

In a hollow where it rains more than it snows, where it rains in fact two days out of three, Juneau is a veritable island-oasis surrounded by sea and icy desert.

Other towns founded in the gold rush era rapidly faded into ghost towns after the gold mines were abandoned. Two factors have saved Juneau from this fate. For some reason, unlike the other rip-roaring mining towns, it never suffered a major downtown fire, so that many of its old buildings from before World War I still stand intact. In addition, the fact of state government gave Juneau another *raison d'être* beyond the ephemeral attraction of gold mining. As a result, the town has retained a certain quaint charm lacking in the ferocious modernity of Alaska's other large towns.

The people (about 21,000) are a friendly and unpretentious mix of government officials, shopkeepers, restaurateurs and others whose roots have been pulled up from the states of "the lower 48" to be replaced here temporarily or permanently. Some make an occasional side-trip up to the oil pipeline to make some extra money fast, bring it back, drink, smoke and live it up and take off again. Juneau has a colourful young band of what in the '60's were called hippies and at any time are the more or less carefree drifters that are an essential enlivening element of any frontier society like Alaska.

A Brief History

Up to 1880	Gastineau Channel area inhabited by Auk Indians who fished for salmon in the creeks around the future site of Juneau. On October 4, 1880, Dick Harris and Joe Juneau stake their first gold claim at "Gold Creek".
1881–1900	1881: miners hold first political convention to send customs collector Mottrom D. Ball to Washington as their "delegate to the Congress". Boom years of the gold rush. 1882: great Treadwell Mine built across channel on Douglas Island. 1900: Juneau is incorporated as first-class city.
1900–1930	Alaska's capital moved from Sitka to Juneau prior to convening of territorial legislature in 1913. Lumbering and salmon and halibut fisheries added to gold mining as major industries.
1930 on	Territorial legislature, working towards statehood, builds its first Federal and Territorial Building in Juneau in 1931. The Alaska-Juneau Gold Mine, once the world's largest in terms of daily tonnage, closed down by U.S. government in 1944 to conserve manpower for national war effort. 1959: Juneau becomes capital of U.S.A.'s new 49th state. 1974: Alaska votes to move the capital out of Juneau. For lack of funds, the capital stays put.

Gold Rush?

Never was gold more reluctantly discovered than the stuff that founded the town of Juneau. The fellows who stumbled on it had to be practically dragged kicking and screaming to actually take it out of the ground. The real *rush* began only with those who had a more clear-headed idea of what it represented.

Georg Pilz, a German-born entrepreneur in Sitka, had been looking for men to investigate the source of glittering rock samples brought him in 1879 by the Auk Indian chief Kowee from the Gastineau Channel. The best Pilz could come up with were Dick Harris from Philadelphia, whom he described as "an inveterate drunkard", and Quebec-born Joe Juneau, of whom he said: "Between hooch and squaws, he never had a cent to get away on."

For $4 a day and the rights to two out of every three stakes they made, Harris and Juneau set out from Sitka in July, 1880, with some Auk Indian guides (working for $1 a day and the promise of 100 Hudson Bay blankets if they struck pay-dirt).

The two Americans worked their way north-east and holed up in an Auk village for three weeks of carousing. It was there they made a discovery that enriched the American vocabulary rather than their boss back in Sitka—"hooch", the mind-boggling liquor distilled from boiled ferns by the Hutsunuwa tribe. In one month they had used up their three months' supplies, lost their boat into the bargain and had to struggle back to Sitka via the Gastineau Channel.

Streams of water cascaded into the channel through clefts in the mountains on either side. At one such stream, the Indian guides urged Harris and Juneau to stop to pan for gold. They found 100 pounds of "very good float gold quartz" but staked no claims. Back in Sitka, Chief Kowee was furious and insisted that Pilz send the two drunks back out in September to the headquarters of what finally became known as "Gold Creek".

There, the erosion of glacier and rapids had left what Harris described as "streaks running through the rocks and little lumps as large as peas or beans". These streaks and peas and beans were the harbingers of Alaska's multi-million-dollar gold bonanza.

Harris finally pulled himself together to stake out some claims and give his name to the first township built around the site. But his shady dealings in land-titles prompted other miners to change the name from Harrisburg to Rockwell, in honour of the commander of the local U.S. Navy base overseeing law and order, before plumping for the name of Harris's chum, Juneau.

They both died penniless.

Sightseeing

The sights begin before you reach Juneau. Cruising up the broad Stephens Passage, you'll pass through **icebergs** floating out of Endicott Arm, a 30-mile-long fjord extending north-west from Dawes Glacier. Those bergs have tumbled into Endicott's peaceful waters from Fords Terror, a side-fjord of vicious tides and treacherous ice that have crushed many a boat venturing too far upriver.

More **fjords** indent the coast up to Gastineau Channel—Tracy Arm, Port Snettisham and Taku Inlet, the broadest of them at the southern end of Douglas Island.

Douglas Island, now a prosperous residential suburb connected to Juneau by a narrow bridge, was the site of the great Treadwell Mine. In the 40 years from 1882 to 1922, the mine, nicknamed the Glory Hole, churned out $67 million worth of gold bullion after Pierre Joseph Eruard or "French Pete", as he was known, sold his claim to John Treadwell for not more than $400—some say it was only $5.

The climate in Juneau is indeed milder than the rest of Alaska, but that's a relative concept. The town is built long and narrow to fend off the winds. Along the winding streets that lead up the mountainside from the main central city area, you can't help noticing the hand-rails to hold on to when the gales blow in off the Taku Glacier in winter. The streets often end in wooden stairways when the slope just gets too steep for wheels.

The **Alaska State Museum** (south of Willoughby Avenue) has a good display of Indian folklore and artifacts of the Tlingit, Athabascan and Haida tribes, and collections of the culture of the Aleuts and Eskimos who make up Alaska's reinvigorated native populations. The constant mobility of the white American communities to and from the "lower 48" makes the "native" concept a still valid and necessary factor in understanding. Alaskan life. There are also fine displays of historical memorabilia from the Russian and pioneer days. An audio-visual show, *The Alaska Story,* links all the museum's elements in an impressive account of the state's history.

213 Seventh Street is the House of Wickersham, once an informal museum of Alas-

kan folklore and history but now closed. It was the home of Judge James H. Wickersham, a pioneer legislator who travelled around the territory for 39 years, collecting mementos of Alaskan life.

Across Gold Creek is Evergreen Cemetery, where Joe Juneau and Dick Harris are buried. Nearby is the monument to Chief Kowee, the Indian leader who kept so persistently on the trail of the two reluctant gold hunters.

Indians who were converted to Christianity in Juneau's early days went to **St. Nicholas Orthodox Church,** standing on 5th Street since 1893. In Alaska, that's very old. The octagonal roof has a rather nice belfry and onion-domed cupola. Inside the church are vestments and religious books from the old Russian colony.

There are two entertaining relics of the grand old gold-mining days. One is the **Last Chance Basin,** once the messhall of the Alaska-Juneau Gold Mine and still offering a summertime salmon bake and mining museum. The other is right downtown on Franklin Street, the original gold-diggers' hang-out, the **Red Dog Saloon,** floor awash in sawdust and peanut-shells, honky-tonk piano banging out rowdy songs for everyone to join in. Cool beer or a lusty rye whiskey will wash down your mammoth "poor boy" sandwich.

While in the area, you can obtain tourist literature from the Visitors Information Kiosk at Marine Park. Maps of Juneau are available from the Information Centre in the Davis Log Cabin at 134 Seward Street. This will enable you to cover Juneau's four other major shopping centres, apart from the downtown area itself. Two are next to the airport, the third is at the start of the Mendenhall Loop Road and the fourth is in the Lemon Creek area.

There are more than 20 different hiking trails, and either the Juneau Chamber of Commerce or the U.S. Forest Service will have details of them all. One 20-minute hike to the Mt. Roberts Trail Observation Point gives you a panoramic view. Behind the town is the scenic Mt. Juneau Waterfall, which tumbles 3,600 ft. from the mountain to Gold Creek, now the site of a popular salmon bake.

Juneau is renowned for its salmon fishing. One event in August draws visitors from all over the world—the three-day Golden North Salmon Derby.

Anyone can take part, with the chance of winning a $5,000 prize for the largest king salmon caught.

Outside Town

Eaglecrest, Juneau's fine ski area 14 miles from downtown, offers scores of 'nature-carved' trails.

Excursions out of town mean above all a glimpse of the glaciers. The closest contact you can have here with the fabled "frozen north" is a drive around the loop road of the Glacier Highway to the **Mendenhall Glacier,** 13 miles outside Juneau. Named after a U.S. Coastal Surveyor, Thomas Corwin Mendenhall, the blue and white glacier is 12 miles long and its terminus is 1½ miles wide. It ends with a wall of ice between 100 and 200 feet high in Mendenhall Lake. The lake has been there only since the 1930s, left by the glacier which is receding at a rate of 90 feet per year. In

JUNEAU

fact, the U.S. Forest Service's Visitor Centre stands on ground reclaimed from the re-treating glacier only in 1940. In addition to the plant and tree life springing up in the wake of the glacier, you'll notice that many Juneau residents have chosen to build homes there for a front-row view of the icy phenomenon.

Your Mendenhall trip will also take you to the delightful **Auke Lake** and Chapel-by-the-Lake with its old organ to accompany a moment's meditation.

Most spectacular of all is a flight beyond Mount Juneau and Mount Roberts to the magnificent **Juneau Icefield.** This vast field of glacial activity covering 1,215 square miles is an unending source of research for geologists, botanists, biologists and meteorologists. To the east along the Canadian Yukon frontier is a glittering ridge of mountains that reach their highest peak with the 8,584-foot, four-clawed Devil's Paw at the south-eastern edge.

The icefield has over 30 valley glaciers and the largest of them is the **Taku Glacier,** with its tributary or, as the experts call it, a distributary lobe, the **Hole-in-the-Wall Glacier.** The Hole-in-the-Wall can be visited during a stopover at Taku Lodge, in its idyllic setting near the rain forest. The 30-mile-long Taku is not only the biggest glacier in the Juneau Icefield; it is also the only one which is advancing rather than retreating. The experts estimate that by about the year 2010 the glacier will have dammed up the Taku Inlet to create a huge new ice-locked lake.

That may sound very impressive, but the inexorable advance of the Taku and Hole-in-the-Wall glaciers has also meant that it has been impossible to construct a road linking Juneau to the Alaska River Valley. Still, it gives Juneau a unique tranquillity.

SKAGWAY

Alaska, U.S.A.

Introduction

Skagway's only reason for existing was that it was a place from which you could get to somewhere else. More specifically to where the money was, the $300 million worth of gold dug up at Klondike in the Yukon from 1897 to 1900.

About 70 miles north of Juneau by sea, Skagway offered the shortest but not the easiest route to the gold fields. It simply seemed too tiresome—and too expensive—to take the longer but safer route further north from Norton Sound up the Yukon River, which might freeze over any-

way before you got to the pay-dirt. So it was lucky that pioneer William Moore had discovered the White Pass route through the Coast Mountains above the mouth of the Lynn Canal.

Skagway, derived from a local Indian dialect, happens to mean—very accurately—"home of the North Wind", but that didn't deter thousands of prospectors from flocking up there to try their luck either through White Pass or along the shorter, steeper Chilkoot Pass. Beyond the mountains there was still a 500-mile trek to Klondike.

In those days, Skagway be-

Teach Yourself Gold Digging

Now that the market price of gold has risen high enough for prospecting to be a profitable enterprise once more, people are beginning to look around Alaska again for more of that yellow stuff. If you want to know how to dig for yourself, here's a short course: first dig with a pick and shovel. Dump the pay-dirt—sand, gravel, clay and, you hope, gold —into a flat-bottomed iron or tin pan. Wet and stir. Pick out rocks and pebbles. Rotate the pan gently for 10 minutes under water, holding it slightly aslant so that the clay and most of the sand washes away. Gold, being heavier, remains at the bottom of your pan. Suddenly, you're rich.

Skagway clings to its image of a pioneering, gold-miners' town.

SKAGWAY

came overnight the biggest town in Alaska—20,000 "stampeders", as they were known, who just as quickly disappeared when the glittering stuff ran out in Klondike and the miners moved on to the new finds in Nome. Today, Skagway's a sleepy town of 768 hardy souls, who lovingly preserve the memory of the golden era. Broadway, the main street, is still unpaved, with boardwalks in place of pavements, its turn-of-the-century clapboard hotel, saloons and general stores still in good repair.

When the planks of the boardwalk and the buildings' façades are weathered away by the fierce winters, the townspeople carefully replace each plank. By not applying too much varnish or paint, the town has astutely kept its pioneering aspect. A ghost town with live, lively inhabitants.

In its heyday, Skagway was a riotous, rambunctious place of lawlessness and disorder. Food supplies were just brought up the channel by ship and dumped on to the beach. Supreme indignity, the cattle had to swim themselves

Not-So-Soft Soapy

The most notorious of Skagway's many crooks was Jefferson "Soapy" Smith. He earned his nickname by tricking people into buying soap at what they thought was a good price because of the bonus dollar bills they imagined it was wrapped in. The special wrappings in fact went to Soapy's confederates. He took the greenhorns' money in a variety of ways, principally in crooked gambling games, but, if he didn't have the time to spare, quite simply at gunpoint, particularly if they were on their way *back* from Klondike with their pockets full.

A favourite con-game was the telegram service. Newcomers would be encouraged to send a telegram as soon as they stepped off the boat, to let their family know they'd arrived safely, adding $5 for a prepaid reply. But Skagway had no telegraph line. Finally this state of affairs was too much for the few honest townspeople, who egged on surveyor Frank Reid to challenge Soapy to a gun-duel. Both men died. In the Skagway cemetery, Frank Reid is honoured by a big monument, while Soapy has a measly little plot. But, as is the way with so many good guys and bad guys, everybody here has heard of Soapy and almost everybody has forgotten honest Frank.

ashore into the arms of the waiting butchers. Today, things are better ordered, more sedately, with beef and salmon neatly delivered in refrigerated containers.

You can still hear raucous music in the saloons, and painted ladies bare a red-gartered thigh or two, but they're nice ladies who go home to their husbands after work.

In the town's heyday, bandits and brigands strutted the streets, fleecing the unsuspecting newcomers with the rough justice meted out to all in this world who are unsuspecting. Today, the bandits and brigands are played by smiling, moustache-twirling actors at a safe distance behind the footlights of Skagway's theatreshows.

Artefacts such as this make handsome presents—if you can find good ones.

A Brief History

1888	Pioneer William Moore sets up the first white man's house in the Skagway region after finding the White Pass route through the Coast Mountains to the Yukon.
1897	Gold discovered at Klondike brings thousands to Skagway to use the White Pass or Chilkoot Trail routes, the latter starting at Dyea, 7 miles north of Skagway.
1898	Skagway becomes Alaska's largest town, with a population estimated at 20,000, albeit ultimately transient. "Chinook", a sudden warm wind, melts snow on Coast Mountains, causing avalanches on April 3, 1898, killing 43 prospectors near the Chilkoot Pass. Scores more pack-horses are dying all the time because of mistreatment and overloading. Irish-Canadian Michael Heney, with British financiers, starts work on White Pass & Yukon Railroad from Skagway to Whitehorse (Canada). The mountain railway is completed in an astonishing 14 months.
1899	Gold rush up at Nome on the Bering Sea and dwindling gold stocks at Klondike divert traffic away from Skagway. But the Klondike rush is in general credited with opening up the Alaska territory to thousands of Americans who had previously given no thought to Alaska after Congress had neglected its development in the 30 years since acquisition. (Many Americans at the time think Klondike is part of Alaska.)
1940's	Skagway becomes of renewed importance in World War II as a supply base for the construction of the Alaska Highway, a vital logistic supply-line after the Japanese have captured three of the Aleutian Islands in 1942–43.
1960's	Skagway serves as shipping point for Yukon minerals —lead-zinc concentrates, asbestos and copper—from Whitehorse and the Keno Hills. This gives the old White Pass & Yukon Railroad a new lease of life.

Sightseeing

Star of the historic Broadway downtown area is the grand old **Golden North Hotel.** Built in 1898, it was literally turned around at right angles six years later to face the main street and a distinctive dome was added to its roof. Today it is a living museum of Skagway's great past, each room furnished with authentic pieces of the Klondike period and the walls covered with photos of the old "stampeders" lining up with their poor horses and sleds in the snows of White Pass and Chilkoot Trail.

Saloons along Broadway and on the waterfront can be heard banging out honky tonk music while they pour a rye whiskey considerably better than the gut-rot doled out by the fleecers of the time, most infamous of whom was Jefferson (Soapy) Smith.

Close by the harbour, you can see the weird **Arctic Brotherhood Hall,** where they used to stage melodramatic re-enactments of the Soapy Smith sagas. Its façade is stuck all over with thousands of pieces of driftwood, giving it a marvellously weather-beaten look. On second thoughts, the

Jack London in Skagway

One of the great figures to pass through Skagway during the Klondike gold rush in 1898 was Jack London, legendary California writer, oyster-pirate, socialist and gold-prospector.

In his greatest dog story, *The Call of the Wild,* he evokes the atmosphere of Skagway during the roistering days of the stampeders. The Canadian mail dispatchers Perrault and François reach Skagway with a team of huskies.

"It was a record run. Each day for 14 days they had averaged 40 miles. For three days Perrault and François threw chests up and down the main street of Skagway and were deluged with invitations to drink, while the team was the constant centre of a worshipful crowd of dog-busters and mushers. Then three or four western bad men aspired to clean out the town, were riddled like pepper-boxes for their pains, and public interest turned to other idols."

whole town doesn't just look weather-beaten, it *is* weather-beaten.

The **White Pass & Yukon Railroad** has two dockside terminals, one for freight, one for passengers. Although the railroad has not been in ope-

134

ration for the past couple of years, the well-maintained original coach cars and engines can be seen at the terminal point at the back of town. Perhaps soon the narrow-gauge railroad will return to its former glory as one of the region's great tourist attractions, shuffling passengers over the famous White Pass to Lake Bennett and back. It's enough to make you dream of the gold that was once in them-thar-hills.

Railway to El Dorado

In its own little way, the building of the White Pass & Yukon Railway was at the time a technological exploit worthy of the later Trans-Alaska Pipeline. For the gold prospectors, it served the same purpose—a lifeline for getting to and bringing out the riches being gouged out of the Klondike.

The iron horse of the railway was to replace the sad four-legged variety previously used to haul equipment over the mountains—as one stampeder with a literary turn of mind described them, "ambulatory boneyards, the infirm, the decrepit, those afflicted with spavin and springhalt, and many with ribs like the sides of a whiskey cask and hips to hang hats on."

Starting in the summer of 1898, many of the men bound for the Klondike paused to earn some subsistence money by working on the railway. A few months later, most of them deserted the construction to rush to Atlin, 60 miles east of Skagway, following reports of a rich gold strike there. Many came back empty-handed and resumed work on the railway. The following summer it reached Lake Bennett, where many of the workers once again deserted, this time to build boats to continue north up the lake to the gold fields, too impatient to wait for the railway to reach Whitehorse. Some of the more sentimental types even missed their old horses. After all, if the train broke down on the way over the mountains, you couldn't eat it.

VALDEZ

Alaska, U.S.A.

Introduction

Tucked away in the north-eastern corner of Prince William Sound, Valdez is a place where things tend to fall into its lap, sometimes good, sometimes bad. Three words tell its story—gold, earthquake and oil. As good luck goes, two out of three's not bad going.

Today, as the marine tanker terminal of the already fabled Trans-Alaska Pipeline, Valdez is economically one of the most important places in the state. The ice-free port ships Alaska's North Slope oil out to Seattle, to Japan and through the Panama Canal to all points beyond. Valdez is the culminating point of what Alaskans proudly claim to be the greatest man-made achievement of private enterprise the world has ever known—the Great Wall of China and Egypt's Pyramids being state-run undertakings. As it is, they've laid nearly 800 miles of pipe across three mountain ranges, under 350 rivers and streams, and through active earthquake country where temperatures range from 60° F below zero to 100° above.

A Spanish explorer left his name on the bay, Puerto de Valdéz, at the end of the 18th century, but it was ignored by Americans until a hundred years later when some more good old treasure-hunters chose it as the ideal jumping-off place for the goldfields around Fairbanks. Not being great Spanish-speakers, they pronounced it Val-deez. It stuck.

During the early 1900's Valdez had its little boom as a supply port for Fairbanks, shipping in goods from Seattle. But otherwise 20th-century life was quiet for the few hundred residents.

Till half past five on Good Friday afternoon, March 27, 1964, when the historic earthquake, 8.5 on the Richter scale, smashed the town to smithereens. The waterfront, said eyewitnesses, looked "as though it was sawed off", houses were "snapped from foundations and shredded into kindling".

The destruction of Valdez was so total—with miraculously few casualties—that it was decided simply to rebuild a whole new town four miles to the west on geologically safer ground, with a new harbour for small craft and more substantial docks for ships.

The quiet life returned again, for just four years, until another shock of seismic proportions hit the town, this time a benign one. From the other end of Alaska came news that gigantic oil fields had been discovered on the North Slope and the closest ice-free port was dear old VAL-deez. Jackpot.

New prosperity was guaranteed, but what was the town going to *look* like with all these storage-tanks, power plants and pipes? With its snow-capped mountains and green meadows, locals called the region the "Switzerland of Alaska". Well, you'll judge for yourself, but somehow the Alaska landscape seems miraculously powerful enough to take the terminal in its stride. If not Switzerland, then Valdez is most certainly the Alaska of Alaska.

A Brief History

1790	Fjord is named Puerto de Valdéz during Spanish exploration of Prince William Sound.
1898	Settled by Americans as Alaska's northernmost ice-free port, giving relatively rapid access to Yukon gold fields.
1900's	U.S. Army base is established during town's boom years as supply-port for Fairbanks. General Wilds Richardson constructs the 365-mile Valdez Trail, subsequently turned into Richardson Highway, Alaska's first paved highway.
1916	Valdez hotbed of statehood campaign. *The Forty-Ninth Star* newspaper is founded in Valdez by local boy, Senator Oliver Hubbard. "Subscribe for this paper," it says, "and stand by it until the 49th Star is placed upon that banner of freedom."
1959	The new state of Alaska's first governor is another local boy, William Egan, Valdez general merchandise store-keeper.
1964	Earthquake destroys Valdez. New town is built on geologically sounder ground 4 miles further west.
1968–74	With discovery of North Slope oil fields at Prudhoe Bay, Valdez is chosen as port-outlet for Trans-Alaska Pipeline's marine tanker terminal. Construction begins in 1974 and population rises from 1,200 to 8,000.
1977	First oil through the pipeline reaches Valdez July 28.

One Boy's Earthquake

Simultaneously with the earthquake came a gigantic *tsunami*, a seismic sea-wave, which picked up boats in the bay and dashed them against the mountainside. Good Friday being a holiday, 12-year-old Freddie Christofferson had spent the afternoon watching the Seattle freighter *Chena* unloading its cargo onto the docks. Just as he left, he recalled, "the earth started shaking. When I looked back, I saw the ship up in the air. The water was up on the dock. Then the ship blew the whistle and pushed off. The dock went up in the air after the ship left. It just exploded in a lot of planks. I never did see any of the people on it when it happened."

Sightseeing

Yes, the **marine tanker terminal** is *the* tourist attraction in Valdez, a technological wonder set against the stunning background of the Chugach Mountains, and the history of its construction makes a fascinating story.

Tour buses with entertaining and very knowledgeable guides as drivers take you along the Richardson Highway to visit the whole vast complex—the berths for the gigantic tankers moored in Valdez Bay, the storage tank-farms, the ballast treatment facility, the pipeline itself.

But how did the pipeline and its oil get there anyway?

Too Cold, Too Far Away

In the middle of the 19th century, Eskimos told Russian and American traders strange stories of the black lakes they'd found burning in the Arctic night. But these fellows were in the fur business and the petrol-driven internal combustion engine hadn't yet been invented.

In 1886 a U.S. Navy exploration of the Arctic coast found oil on the North Slope at Colville River, but nothing more was done about it until 1923 when President Warren Harding set up a Naval Petroleum Reserve. Other oil had been found around Barrow in 1921 when Standard Oil of California took a desultory interest in a few oil-seepages. After World War II, private contractors drilled around the Naval Petroleum Reserve, but none of the hundred or so wells was commercially exploitable. Then, in 1957, Atlantic Richfield found oil on the Kenai Peninsula and suddenly other big oil companies began to take Alaska seriously.

Ten years before the oil-rush began, a land boom developed as the state raked in $66,000,000 in land leases for the most promising oil fields. At that time, oilmen didn't want to consider the North Slope around Prudhoe Bay because it was felt to be too cold and too far away.

Finally, half-heartedly, Atlantic Richfield started drilling on the first of two North Slope leases, at Saganavirktok River. Luckily, the oil was found in the other, more easily pronounceable place, Prudhoe Bay, Atlantic Richfield confirming in 1968 that there were "significant" amounts of oil down there.

Roll out the Barrels

Geologists in Fairbanks were less modest than the oil-company people; they said the North Slope oil fields were "evidently mammoth" and "almost certainly of Middle-Eastern proportions". To keep things in proportion, the North Slope proved to have estimated reserves of 9,600 million barrels of oil, which is a lot, but Saudi Arabia alone has 165,000 million barrels—17 times as much. A barrel, by the way is 42 U.S. gallons, 35 British.

Valdez, Here We Come!

The moment the news broke, Alaska had to brace itself for a whole new generation of stampeders—Texans in stetson hats and high boots, New York bankers in pinstripe suits, and Houston bankers in pinstripe suits *with* stetson and boots. On September 10, 1969 they gathered in Fairbanks for the North Slope land lease sale. The state of Alaska raked in a 20 per cent cash down payment on $900,220,590, bid in the space of seven hours. The money was immediately bagged and flown out of town to a San Francisco bank to start earning its interest that very day.

That same month, steel pipe from Japan was unloaded at Valdez for the grand Trans-Alaska Pipeline jointly planned by Atlantic Richfield, British Petroleum and Humble Oil to move hot oil 789 miles from Prudhoe Bay to the Pacific Ocean. The pipe was Japanese because no American company made the 48-inch-diameter pipe necessary to deliver the projected 2 million barrels a day. The oil would be hot—135° F—so as to be still pumpable during winter shutdowns when it might be 60° below zero outside.

Not so fast, said the conservationists. A buried hot-oil pipeline might melt the permafrost, that permanently frozen soil beneath the surface that is an essential feature of the Alaskan ecosystem. And an above-ground pipeline will block caribou in their seasonal migrations. Construction will destroy fish-spawning grounds and forests. And what about the risk of oil-leakage? This is earthquake country. And even if the oil gets safely through the pipeline, what about the risks of oil spills at sea when the tankers confront the icebergs on Prince William Sound?

Not so fast, said the Eskimos, Indians and Aleuts, too. This pipeline will cross *our* land.

So the oil companies had to set to work to solve the environmental problems and even to help lobby in Washington for the Native Land Claims Settlement Act or else their pipeline would never get to make it all the way to Valdez.

The Alyeska Pipeline Service Company, as the consortium's construction firm became known, modified and refined its technology to meet the conservationists' objections (originally estimated at

$900 million, the pipeline finally cost $7,700 million). The Eskimos, Indians and Aleuts got their land-claim settlement. And the Arabs imposed an oil embargo after the Yom Kippur War against Israel in October 1973. In November 1973, Congress authorized the pipeline.

After checking with Valdez that it was ready to receive its first offering, Prudhoe Bay pumped the first crude oil down the pipeline on June 20, 1977—nine years after the North Slope oil field was activated.

There was a series of near and actual calamities. A vehicle crashed into the pipe after the flow had begun, but damage was repaired before the oil reached the ruptured section. It was halted by a (false) earthquake alarm. A pump station south of Fairbanks exploded, killing one worker and injuring five others. After a ten-day halt, the pipeline by-passed the destroyed station and the oil-flow resumed. A damaged valve sprang a leak that spread 2,000 barrels of oil over the tundra south of Prudhoe Bay before it could be repaired. Finally, the first oil reached the Valdez tanker terminal 38 days, 12 hours and 58 minutes after it started. (A lady named Jean Mahoney won $30,000 in a lottery for guessing the right time within 60 seconds.)

Shoes and Pigs

The pipeline is built to withstand an 8.5-Richter earthquake, like the one that destroyed Valdez in 1964. At regular intervals, Teflon-coated "shoes" can slide the elevated pipe on support beams during tremors. The line zigzags through the landscape to minimize ruptures. Gate-valves close down within four minutes of a hitch at river-crossings and other "environmentally sensitive" areas (but it could still spill 15,000 barrels during that time). In regions crossed by migrating caribou, the pipes are buried 3 to 12 feet underground. While fibreglass and polyurethane insulate the hot oil inside the pipe, liquid ammonia or a heat-absorbant sand-and-water mixture known as slurry cools the pipe's exterior so as not to melt the permafrost.

But nicest gadget of all is the "batching pig" which precedes the oil down the pipeline. This little pig goes to Valdez with a little wheel emitting a "squeal" so that tracking teams can locate the oil-front. It even has a radio-transmitter to provide checks for leaks, heat-stress and pipe-waggle.

Anti-Pipe Dreams

Faced with the opposition to the pipeline, the oil companies came up with some other bizarre ideas for moving the oil. A huge *super-tanker* was fitted with extra-strong ice-breakers to navigate the North-West Passage to the Pacific, but ice nevertheless broke a hole in the hull "big enough to drive a truck through" and the experiment was abandoned. Boeing suggested a *flying tanker,* equipped with 12 Jumbo 747 jet engines and a wing span of 478 feet. Others proposed adapting 900-foot *nuclear-powered submarines* to carry 300,000 tons of oil. Finally, Mark Wheeler, a Ketchikan cartoonist, came up with the most plausible alternative: a 789-mile *human chain* passing the oil from Prudhoe Bay to Valdez in buckets.

Sightseeing at the Valdez Marine Tanker Terminal

At the terminal itself, you'll see four main *berths* in the bay where the tankers ranging from 16,000 to 265,000 tons arrive for their oil cargo. They first empty the water ballast from the hold (serving to keep them stable while at sea without the oil cargo) through pipes into the *ballast treatment facility.* The ballast tanks purify the slightly oily water to proper environmental standards and discharge it into the bay 700 feet offshore 200 feet down.

The tankers then take on their cargo from the crude oil storage *tank farms.* Each of the 18 tanks is 250 feet in diameter, 62 feet high, holding 510,000 barrels. Concrete dikes surround the tanks to contain the oil if the tanks spring a leak. The whole place is of course swarming with firefighting systems.

The *Operations Control Centre* controls the whole 789-mile pipeline, directing oil into the storage tanks and out again to the waiting tankers.

You can survey the whole complex from a *visitors' observation post.* Beyond it, you see Valdez Bay, the spruce forests, the white snows. There are black bears in the forests and mountains, and goats, moose, deer and beaver. In Prince William Sound, whale, porpoise and seal.

ANCHORAGE

Alaska, U.S.A.

Introduction

"Anchorage, Alaska, uncontrolled mosaic". No better description could be found for this tough, energetic town that has sprouted up on a peninsula at the head of Cook Inlet, hemmed in by the Talkeetna Mountains to the north and the Chugach to the east.

Its development is a classically rugged American story. Founded seventy years ago as a tent-city to encamp workers for the Alaska Railroad—an "anchorage" for the supply ships from Seattle—it grew up as a military base in World War II and then became the major seaport and commercial centre for the state's oil and gas industries.

It is now the fastest-growing city in Alaska, with a booming economy. Tourism is the state's second-largest industry, and Anchorage Airport handles more international traffic than any other city of its size in the world. Whittier, the port for Anchorage, provides some breathtaking alpine scenery for visitors using the rail connection, with its delightful domed observation cars.

Since Anchorage is where the money is, it's also where top executives gather in dimly lit hotel bars and smoke-filled boardrooms to hammer out decisions which will be voted on in Juneau—capital of Alaska, but only on sufferance. The decisions made for Anchorage itself are brutally efficient. In 1964, when an earthquake totally destroyed the downtown business district, the rebuilders just paved over most of the devastated area for a huge car park and put up a new high-rise construction on its periphery. Uncontrolled mosaic.

No time for sentimental urban planning. Anchorage is the starting point and terminus of modern industrial Alaska. All the roads, railways and air-routes either begin or end here. It's built like a no-nonsense communications and transportation centre, with a few elegant neighbourhoods for the city's managers.

Today it is the most "American" of Alaska's cities, its skyscrapers and grid-plan making it comparable on a smaller scale to Kansas City, Indianapolis or, with that dramatic mountain backdrop, Denver.

The town never quite shakes off the surrounding wilderness. The city is bounded to the west and south by the two fjord-like Knik and Turnagain arms of the Inlet and is divided within the city limits by two swiftly flowing streams, Ship Creek and Chester Creek, both teeming with salmon. On nearby lakes Spenard and Hope, wild birds (principally grebes and loons) maintain an uneasy coexistence with the man-made variety—float-planes of affluent Anchorage residents. (Road and rail are more practical for freight than for passengers, so Anchorage has acquired more private aircraft per capita than anywhere else in the world.) In the winter, a special city ordinance provides right of way through the city streets for wild moose.

But only a small minority in this busy, busy town is conscientious about protecting the natural environment. The editor of the *Anchorage Times* is on record as having said: "Idealists here in town see a need for a park in every housing development. They favour animals, trees, water, flowers. Who ever makes a plan for man?"

Meanwhile, the idealists have at least managed to preserve the local Chugach State Park covering about 30 square miles (78 sq.km.) at the western edge of the gigantic Chugach National Forest. The park provides facilities for hiking, bird-watching and camping.

Anchorage prides itself on its role as "America's last frontier town" and people dress accordingly in cowboy boots and stetsons, even though the only heifers and longhorns around are in the deep-freezes of the big steakhouses. Otherwise the pioneer ambience is sustained in the clubs blaring out country-and-western music and in the seedy saloons of the red-light district along 4th Avenue. You might run into a high-stakes poker game pitching old oilmen against young real-estate pedlars who estimate the odds on pocket calculators. Dodge City with new dodges.

A Brief History

18th century	In 1778 Captain James Cook explores the inlet—Cook Inlet—where Anchorage now stands.
20th century	A construction camp is established in 1914 for labourers working on the Alaska Railroad, with an "anchorage" for freighters on Ship Creek. The tent-city is eventually replaced in 1920 by a properly constituted township

with its first municipal government. By 1923, the Alaska Railroad is completed and Anchorage well established as a supply centre for nearby farmers, miners and trappers.

After the German occupation of Norway and Denmark in World War II, just across the North Pole from Alaska, Anchorage becomes an important military base, reinforced after the Japanese invasion of Alaska's Aleutian Islands in 1942. Anchorage's strategic role becomes more significant during the Cold War when Fort Richardson and Elmendorf Air Force Base are established to monitor Soviet movements, evolving into today's U.S. Polar Defense Headquarters.

An earthquake in 1964 leaves 2,000 homeless and completely destroys the downtown business district and several residential areas. Sales of North Slope oil-lands bring in over $900 million during just seven hours' bidding for 450,000 acres (182,000 hectares).

The oil boom in the 1970s engenders a population explosion with an increase from 48,000 in 1970 to 180,000 by the end of the decade.

Sightseeing

Not even the most fervent Anchorage booster would claim that his city was pretty—he'd probably suggest pretty cities are for sissies—but he'd justifiably punch you on the nose if you didn't appreciate the beauty of its natural setting. To do justice to the **view**, there are some good vantage points in rooftop restaurants and bars in the major hotels. You can take in the whole peninsula and the Knik and Turnagain fjords. To the east, you see the peaks of the Chugach Mountains—Temptation, Wolverine, Suicide, Tanaina—with houses (some of them chalets, some ranch-style) lighting up the mountainsides in the evening to remind Californians of the Hollywood Hills.

You also get an awesome view, 125 miles (200 km.) to the north, of **Mount McKinley**, at 20,320 feet (6,194 metres) the tallest mountain in North America. This crown of the Alaska Range—and indeed of the whole chain of Rockies that extends down to Mexico—is known to the Eskimos and Indians quite simply as Denali, The Great One, a name gradually reasserting itself over that of the not very distinguished former American president. The mountain commands a 3,000-square-mile (7,770-sq.-km.) national park much prized by naturalists for its caribou, moose, wolf and Toklat grizzly bear, but less so for the mosquitoes that infest the area in summer. The mountain was first conquered in 1913 by the Reverend Hudson Stuck, London-born archdeacon of the Yukon.

Closer at hand, **Chugach State Park** will give you the opportunity to see some of the animals that roam the Chugach Mountains. Most common is the handsome wild Dall sheep. The ram's spectacu-

Apex of the continent, the snowy summit of Mt. McKinley can be seen from Anchorage.

lar golden curved horns measure up to 40 inches (over a metre) in length, with growth rings indicating, like the cross-section of a tree trunk, the beast's age. Mountain goats have beautiful pure white shaggy coats and a terrific Karl-Marx-like beard. With a little luck you may spot a lynx among the trees. This cat is the size of a Great Dane and its famous eyes are bright yellow. You may even see a muskrat out on a ramble. In season refresh yourself with the delicious wild blueberries.

If you want a closer look at the animals, go out to **Alaska Zoo** on O'Malley Road, 2 miles (3 km.) off the Seward Highway. In a natural parkland and wooded setting of 8 acres (3 hectares), you can see up to 40 different species of the wildlife that inhabit this biggest of American states.

Elmendorf Air Base north of the town has a nicely arranged **Wildlife Museum** for more leisurely study of the region's big game and wild birds.

Earthquake Park, at the west end of Northern Lights Boulevard, is a strange and fascinating display covering 132 acres (53 hectares) of what was once a smart residential area and is now a twisted, gutted mass of earth-mounds and smashed trees left by the 1964 earthquake. The manner in which nature is reclaiming this land over the years gives the devastation a bizzare, almost perverse new beauty.

Native arts and crafts, Aleut, Indian and Eskimo tools, weapons and traditional costumes are exhibited at the **Historical and Fine Arts Museum,** an attractively designed low-slung rectangular building at 121 West 7th Avenue. The stylized totemic frieze along the exterior corniche is by local Alaskan artist Alex Duff Combs, whose fine sculpture you can also see beside the Anchorage Natural Gas Building at the corner of Spenard Road and 31st Street.

If you're looking for authentic native craftwork to buy, try the gift shop at the **Alaska Arctic Indian and Eskimo Museum,** 819 West 4th Avenue. There's an ivory workshop on the premises where you can see local artisans carving jewellery and sculpture from whale teeth and walrus tusks.

The saga of Eskimo and Indian hunters, Russian fur traders, American gold-diggers and Texan pipe-liners can be seen in the audio-visual show, **Alaska Story,** projected

daily at the Captain Cook Hotel.

Down at the waterfront, **Turnagain Arm** provides a splendidly hypnotic natural show at low tide (check the local newspapers for exact times). The tidal change creates a particularly impressive rush of water flowing across the mud flats up the narrow inlet.

If you're not careful, shopping in Anchorage is a hazardous affair among the breathtakingly awful junk in most of the downtown souvenir shops. Be sure to look for the 'Silver Hand' label on the craftwork guaranteeing that it was made by authentic regional craftsmen and not on a conveyor belt in Taiwan or Korea. Best bets are the superb fur jackets and parkas, simple ivory or soapstone carvings, pottery, and gold-nugget or jade jewellery. You may be surprised to find books on sale *by weight*.

Of Cabbages and Queens

Farmers all over the world are forever boasting of miraculous 50-pound cabbages, 6-pound turnips, vegetable marrows as big as a full-grown pig. In the Matanuska Valley immediately north-east of Anchorage and only 350 miles (560 km.) south of the Arctic Circle, these "miracles" are regular facts of life.

Beginning at the market-town of Palmer, the valley has grown out of one of the United States' most ambitious farming projects. It was conceived in the years of the Depression, when Franklin D. Roosevelt's New Dealers were searching for ways of putting the skills and talents of impoverished workers to new advantage. In 1935, the Alaska Relief and Rehabilitation Corporation was set up to manage the Matanuska Valley Colony—a truly colonial project on the European model, minus the exploitation of native labour—of 201 families brought in from Michigan, Minnesota and Wisconsin.

First or second generation immigrants from Norway, Sweden and Finland, they were considered ideally adapted to handling farming in the rigours of Alaska. In fact, agriculturalists were impressed by Matanuska Valley's unusually mild climate for this latitude—warmer in winter than most of the northern states of the "Lower 48"—and with plenty of rain and midnight sun to sustain exceptional growth.

The New Deal's ardent propaganda and the plans for setting up cooperative marketing resulted in right-wing opponents, who sniffed socialism in any federally subsidized project, scorning Matanuska as "Uncle Sam's first collective farm". It did not make anybody inordinately rich, but the fertile valley carved out by the glaciers of the Talkeetna Mountains has produced spectacular results with giant vegetables, all perfectly edible. The record cabbage weighed in at 72 pounds, as much as a fair-sized teenager, and turnips have gone to 8 pounds.

The outsize produce can be seen each year at the autumn Alaska State Fair in Palmer, in early September. The Midsummer Festival in June is highlighted by the Matanuska Valley Pageant. The beauty queen's measurements are invariably impressive, but not abnormal.

SEWARD

Alaska, U.S.A.

Introduction

The glistening white houses of Seward sit on a half-moon of shoreline at the edge of a pine grove that forms the western border of the Chugach National Forest, with the rugged Mount Marathon looming behind it.

The town is by no means the only thing named after William H. Seward, Secretary of State of Abraham Lincoln and his successor Andrew Johnson. The piece of land across the Bering Strait from the Soviet Union is the Seward Peninsula. That's appropriate enough, since it was Seward who negotiated the purchase of Alaska in 1867. By the same token, Alaska itself was for some time known to people who thought the purchase idiotic as "Seward's Folly" or "Seward's Icebox".

The town was founded on the east side of Kenai Peninsula in 1903, some 30 years after the Secretary of State's death. Its advantageous position at the sheltered head of the narrow Resurrection Bay made it an ideal communications centre, both as an ice-free port receiving Alaska's cargo from "outside" and as the ocean terminus of the Alaska Central Railroad to Fairbanks and the interior.

More recently the town's commercial importance has been somewhat overshadowed by the development of Anchorage as the major railroad and port facility of the region. But Seward's attractive natural harbour has made it a favourite sailing and fishing resort for holidaymakers from metropolitan Anchorage 128 miles to the north.

Guts for Galoshes

The Steller Sea Lion, to give him his full name and distinguish him from the California Sea Lion you may have seen performing tricks at the circus, can grow to 13 feet in total length and weigh some 2,400 pounds. Females are rarely more than 7 feet in length and 700 to 800 pounds in weight.

The sea lions' short, coarse fur ranges in colour from light brown to black, though they all start life dark chocolate brown. Their favourite food is herring, salmon, halibut and flounder, from time to time preceded by an *hors d'œuvre* of shrimp or crab. And they themselves occasionally end up on the menu of a passing shark or killer whale. If the Eskimos catch them first, their hides are used for boat-linings and their intestines for waterproof clothing.

A Brief History

18th century

At Resurrection Bay in 1794, Alaska's Russian governor Alexander Baranof launches the *Phoenix*, first ship to be made in Alaska, modelled and named after a British schooner visiting Alaska from Calcutta.

20th century

The town of Seward is founded in 1903 as the future starting-point for the 470-mile Alaska Central Railroad to Fairbanks. The railway is not begun until 1915 and completed in 1923, initially to serve the Matanuska coal-fields.

In old wooden wagons first used in construction of the Panama Canal, the first Matanuska farm-workers set out from Seward in the 1930s.

An economic boom in World War II increases the population from 949 to 2,063 in ten years.

A tsunami (seismic sea-wave) and earthquake hits Seward in 1964.

1970s—
present day

The Alaska oil pipeline brings modernization of the railroad and large-scale investment by the Chugach Natives Inc., the regional corporation of Aleuts and Eskimos who bought up much of the land in and around Seward with money from their land-claims settlement. The population is currently around 3,000.

Sightseeing

To the west of Resurrection Bay is **Bear Glacier,** part of the Harding Icefield that covers 1,500 square miles of the Kenai Mountains.

Further up the bay, look out for **Rugged Island,** home of several hundred sea lions. You may even hear a chorus of sea lion bulls roaring to keep the ship away from the rookery where they stand guard over their harems, each sheltering about 15 wives.

The **harbour,** much favoured by the sailing gentry of Anchorage, is a great place for those who like fine pleasure boats. In mid-August it's the focus of an eight-day round-the-clock Silver Salmon Derby.

Hikers might like at least to walk up the lower slopes of 3,000-foot **Mount Marathon**— on July 4, there's a foot-race all the way to the top.

Laughing All the Way
to the Bank

William H. Seward first attracted national attention when, as Abraham Lincoln's Secretary of State, he was seriously wounded in the assassination plot that cost the President his life. But he is best known as the man who bought Alaska from the Russians for $7,200,000, or two cents an acre, which, when you think of the price of oil today, is not a bad bargain.

Everybody laughed at Seward in 1867 when he was frantically pursuing the Tsar's representatives around Washington to get them to agree to the price. (He didn't know at the time that the Russians were just as eager to be rid of that big chunk of ice.) The great New York newspaperman Horace Greeley advised any Europeans who wanted to dump worthless territory to get in contact with Mr. Seward. Alaska pipeline operators today suggest that, had it been available, Greeley would have advised Israel not to buy Saudi Arabia.

HOMER

Alaska, U.S.A.

Introduction

In a state that has traditionally attracted entrepreneurs, gold-diggers, oil-prospectors, in general the finest or at least most adventurous of America's free enterprise system, Homer has become something of an exception. It's carved for itself the reputation of an artists' colony at the southern end of Kachemak Bay. (*Kachemak* means "smoky" in Aleut, after the smouldering surface coal seams found in the area and still used for winter fuel.)

Originally, like so many other towns along Alaska's Pacific coast, Homer was founded as supply base for fortune-hunters in the Gold Rush at the turn of the century. But after a while, the gold didn't pan out and the dreamers started to look around them at the landscape—the narrow sand bar that stretched 5 miles out into Kachemak Bay, the quivering aspen poplars along the shoreline, the forest of birches and pines, the lupins, fireweed and other colourful wild flowers in the hills and meadows behind the town and, across the bay, the spectacular snow-capped range of the Kenai Mountains. (The mountains provided a welcome barrier to the fierce storms whipping the southwest coast of the peninsula from the Gulf of Alaska.)

This was a natural beauty worth capturing for posterity, the eery northern light bringing out a special brilliance in the colours, the reds and golds of autumn playing kaleidoscopic games with the blue and silver of sea and snow. For any painters with the least bit of frontier spirit, a desire to get well and truly away from it all and not just move a few miles upstate New York in easy commuting distance from their Manhattan "fix", Homer has proved a delightful answer.

And when they get a mild attack of artist's block, they'll go and fish some halibut, king crab or clams from Kachemak Bay. The wild berries that are legion in the surrounding countryside make some excellent jams and preserves for the more sedate members of the community or some mean liqueur and *eau de vie* from a couple of illicit stills tucked away out of sight of the federal authorities.

A Brief History

19th century   Sheltered Kachemak Bay area is popular during the 1850s as a summer resort for Russian fur-traders.

Homer is founded in 1890 by Homer Pennock and his fellow gold-prospectors stocking up for the Yukon gold-fields.

20th century   In 1907 an exposed seam of coal smoulders into a blazing fire and burns down the entire town, except for the Smoky Dawg Saloon.

After six decades of peaceful reconstruction, the whole town is wiped out again in 1964, this time by earthquake—except for the Smoky Dawg Saloon. The population hovers around 2,200.

Sightseeing

The galleries and studios of the artists' colony can be visited, besides in downtown Homer, out at **Anchor Point** and **Halibut Cove.** While you're encouraged to admire and even buy the artwork, you'll frequently find yourself offered free refreshments.

The great historic landmark of Homer is of course the **Smoky Dawg Saloon** on Homer Spit, the 5-mile-long sand bar that was the original site of the gold-rush town. The log-cabin bar, with its boardwalk outside and single-plank name-plate, sits squarely in front of the lighthouse, defying fire and earthquake and providing stiff drinks that have their own hot and even seismic impact.

The **Pratt Museum** displays an interesting array of Russian, Indian and Aleut artefacts from the Kachemak Bay and Cook Inlet region.

Kachemak Bay has proved to be the richest life-producing marine bay in the world. Gull Island is a haven for bird-watchers hunting down Arctic and Pacific species, including long-necked cormorants, puffins and bald eagles. Cruises are organized from Homer harbour in local fishing boats. Look out too for sea otters, sea lions, porpoises and whales.

Alaska Wild Berry Products is a fruit-packing company which welcomes visitors to buy a wonderful range of home-made jams and preserves, ideal for gifts. (The local liquor is not for sale here.) In August, the town stages a Harvest Fair that gives you a good, idea of the ingenious local cooking motivated by being so far from the mass-produced supermarket foods of the "lower 48".

Homer also affords an impressive view of half a dozen major glaciers, the most important being the **Grewingk,** named after the German geologist who first studied it at the beginning of the century. At last count, the Grewingk measured 13 miles in length, but it's receding.

In the hills behind Homer, you may see an occasional brown bear or moose—what Alaska likes to call the world's biggest deer. Moose may look clumsy, with faces not unlike Mickey Mouse's pal Goofy, but they are very fast on their feet and immensely strong and courageous. The cows are even more ferocious than the bulls, especially during the September breeding season. That great flap of flesh hanging underneath their chins is known as a bell—sometimes up to 2 feet in length. Nobody knows what it's for, but we don't advise you to tug it to find out. The bulls have grand sets of antlers—new in May, shed in late November—spanning up to 6 feet from tip to tip.

Index

An asterisk (*) next to a page number indicates a map reference. Where there is more than one set of page references, the one in bold type refers to the main entry.